INVISIBLE IN AMERICA

Invisible in America

The Struggle of the Homeless

Susie Payne

Homeless

CONTENTS

Invisible In America: The Struggle Of The Homeless 1
Copyright 2
Dedication 3
Acknowledgements 4
   1 - The Invisible Epidemic 5
   2 - The Root Causes Of Homelessness 12
   3 - Fictional Story: Terry-The Lifelong Addict . . 22
   4 - Average Minimum Wage 35
   5 - The Challenges Faced By The Homeless Population 39
   6 - Overcoming Homelessness In America 46
   7 - The Role Of Government And Nonprofit Organizations 49
   8 - How Many People Are Homeless In America? 56
   9 - Personal Stories Of Struggle And Resilience 60
   10 - Housing First Approaches 67

11 - Taking Action As Individuals And
    Communities 74
12 - The Future Of Homelessness In America . . . 112
13 - Conclusion 119

Thank You For Reading My Book 123
About The Author 125

INVISIBLE IN AMERICA: THE STRUGGLE OF THE HOMELESS

By Susie Payne

COPYRIGHT

Copyright © 2024 Susie Payne
All rights reserved.
ISBN:

DEDICATION

Inspired by the remarkable tales of forgiveness woven by historical icons such as Nelson Mandela, Mahatma Gandhi, and spiritual luminaries like the Dalai Lama, I dedicate this book. As a woman of profound faith, guided by the teachings of Jesus Christ, I understand the profound impact of truth and justice. My earnest wish is for you to find the courage to be truthful and honest, both with yourself and to others, recognizing that we all may unwittingly inflict harm.

ACKNOWLEDGEMENTS

I am deeply grateful to my loving family, especially my husband of 37 years and my two wonderful children, for their unwavering support and understanding throughout the process of bringing this book to life. Your encouragement and patience have been my rock. To my friends and colleagues who provided invaluable feedback, encouragement, and inspiration along the way, thank you for believing in me and cheering me on. I would also like to express my gratitude to the readers who have embraced my stories with open hearts. Your enthusiasm and support mean the world to me.

1

THE INVISIBLE EPIDEMIC

The Rise of Homelessness in America

In recent years, the issue of homelessness in America has reached unprecedented levels, with more and more individuals and families finding themselves without a place to call home. The rise of homelessness in America can be attributed to a variety of factors, including economic instability, lack of affordable housing, and inadequate support systems for those in need. As a result, millions of Americans are facing the harsh realities of living on the streets or in overcrowded shelters, struggling to survive in an unforgiving world.

One of the most alarming trends in the rise of homelessness in America is the increasing number of families who are experiencing homelessness. According to recent studies, over half of the homeless population in America is made up of families with children. This is a troubling statistic that highlights the impact of economic hardship on families across the country. Many of these families are forced to choose between paying for basic necessities like food and healthcare or keeping a roof over their heads, leading to a cycle of poverty that is difficult to break.

Another contributing factor to the rise of homelessness in America is the lack of affordable housing options. As the cost of living continues to rise, many Americans are finding it increasingly difficult to afford a place to live. This has led to a growing number of individuals and families being pushed out of their homes and onto the streets. Without access to safe and stable housing, these individuals are left vulnerable to the dangers of living on the streets, including violence, substance abuse, and mental health issues.

In addition to economic instability and lack of affordable housing, the rise of homelessness in America can also be attributed to the inadequate support systems in place for those in need. Many homeless individuals struggle to access essential services like healthcare, mental health treatment, and job training programs, leaving them trapped in a cycle of poverty and homelessness. Without proper support and resources, it can be incredibly challenging for homeless individuals to rebuild their lives and find a way out of homelessness.

As the rise of homelessness in America continues to be a pressing issue, it is crucial for Americans to come together to address this crisis and provide support for those in need. By advocating for affordable housing, increased access to essential services, and stronger support systems for homeless individuals, we can work towards ending homelessness in America and ensuring that everyone has a safe and stable place to call home. Together, we can make a difference in the lives of those who are struggling on the streets and help to create a more just and compassionate society for all.

Misconceptions and Stereotypes

Misconceptions and stereotypes surrounding homelessness in America are widespread and deeply ingrained in our society. Many Americans hold the belief that individuals experiencing homelessness are lazy, unmotivated, or somehow deserving of their situation. This harmful stereotype overlooks the systemic issues that contribute to homelessness, such as lack of affordable housing, mental illness, and substance abuse.

One common misconception is that homeless individuals are solely responsible for their predicament. In reality, many people experiencing homelessness have faced a series of unfortunate events, such as job loss, domestic violence, or medical emergencies, that have left them without a stable place to live. It is important for Americans to recognize that homelessness can happen to anyone, regardless of their background or circumstances.

Another prevalent stereotype is that homeless individuals are dangerous or untrustworthy. This belief perpetuates the stigma surrounding homelessness and can prevent individuals from receiving the help and support they need. In truth, the vast majority of people experiencing homelessness are not a threat to society and are simply trying to survive in difficult circumstances.

It is crucial for Americans to challenge these misconceptions and stereotypes surrounding homelessness in order to create a more compassionate and understanding society. By educating ourselves on the root causes of homelessness and advocating for policies that address these issues, we can work towards ending the cycle of poverty and homelessness in America.

The Impact of Homelessness on Individuals and Communities

Homelessness is a pervasive issue that affects individuals and communities across America. The impact of homelessness goes far beyond just the individuals experiencing it, as it also has wide-reaching effects on the communities in which they live. When individuals are forced to live on the streets or in shelters, they face a myriad of challenges that can have lasting effects on their physical and mental well-being. Additionally, the presence of homelessness can have negative effects on the overall health and safety of a community.

For individuals experiencing homelessness, the impact can be devastating. Lack of access to basic necessities such as food, shelter, and healthcare can result in serious health issues. Mental health concerns are also prevalent among the homeless population, as the stress and trauma of living on the streets can take a significant toll on one's mental well-being. Additionally, the lack of stable housing can make it difficult for individuals to maintain employment or access educational opportunities, further perpetuating the cycle of homelessness.

Communities also feel the impact of homelessness in a variety of ways. The presence of homeless individuals can lead to increased crime rates and safety concerns for residents. Additionally, the strain on social services and resources can create challenges for local governments and organizations that are working to support those experiencing homelessness. The visibility of homelessness in a community can also have negative effects on property values and economic development, as potential residents and businesses may be deterred by the presence of homelessness in the area.

Addressing the impact of homelessness on individuals and communities requires a multifaceted approach.

Providing access to affordable housing, mental health services, and employment opportunities are key components of addressing the root causes of homelessness. Additionally, community outreach and support programs can help to foster a sense of belonging and connection for those experiencing homelessness. By working together as a society to address the systemic issues that contribute to homelessness, we can create a more inclusive and supportive environment for all individuals in America.

The Poor Will Always Be Among You

The phrase "The poor will always be among you" originates from biblical scripture, specifically from the Gospel of Matthew in the New Testament. In Matthew 26:11, Jesus responds to disciples who question the use of expensive oil on him, saying, "The poor you will always have with you, but you will not always have me."

The expression suggests that poverty is an enduring and persistent aspect of human society. It implies that it will persist to some degree despite efforts to alleviate poverty. The statement doesn't endorse complacency or indifference toward poverty but recognizes the ongoing challenge of addressing and eradicating poverty.

The Bible contains numerous verses that emphasize God's concern for the poor and marginalized.

Proverbs 14:31 (NIV) "Whoever oppresses the poor shows contempt for their Maker, but whoever is kind to the needy honors God."

Proverbs 19:17 (NIV) "Whoever is kind to the poor lends to the Lord, and he will reward them for what they have done."

Matthew 25:35-36 (NIV) "For I was hungry, and you gave me something to eat, I was thirsty, and you gave me something to drink. I was a stranger, and you invited me in. I needed clothes, and you clothed me, I was sick, and you looked after me, I was in prison, and you came to visit me."

Luke 3:11 (NIV) "John answered, 'Anyone who has two shirts should share with the one who has none, and anyone who has food should do the same.'"

James 2:5 (NIV) "Listen, my dear brothers and sisters: Has not God chosen those who are poor in the eyes of the world to be rich in faith and to inherit the kingdom he promised those who love him?"

James 2:14-17 (NIV) "What good is it, my brothers and sisters, if someone claims to have faith but has no deeds? Can such faith save them? Suppose a brother or a sister is without clothes and daily food. If one of you says to them, 'Go in peace; keep warm and well fed,' but does nothing about their physical needs, what good is it? In the same way, faith by itself, if it is not accompanied by action, is dead."

Proverbs 22:9 (NIV) "The generous will themselves be blessed, for they share their food with the poor."

Psalm 82:3-4 (NIV) "Defend the weak and the fatherless; uphold the cause of the poor and the oppressed. Rescue the weak and the needy; deliver them from the hand of the wicked."

These verses reflect the biblical emphasis on compassion, justice, and care for the poor and marginalized. They encourage believers to extend a helping hand, demonstrating God's love through acts of kindness and generosity.

2

THE ROOT CAUSES OF HOMELESSNESS

Economic Inequality and Housing Affordability

In America, economic inequality is a significant factor contributing to the issue of housing affordability, especially for those who are homeless. The gap between the rich and the poor continues to widen, making it increasingly difficult for low-income individuals and families to afford stable housing. As a result, many individuals find themselves living on the streets or in temporary shelters, struggling to make ends meet. This economic disparity is a major barrier to addressing the homelessness crisis in our country.

The cost of housing in America has skyrocketed in recent years, far outpacing the rate of wage growth for many low-income workers. This has led to a situation where affordable housing is becoming increasingly scarce, forcing many individuals and families to make the difficult choice between paying for housing or other basic necessities. As a result, homelessness rates have continued to rise, particularly in urban areas where housing costs are highest. The lack of affordable housing options is a major contributing factor to the growing homeless population in America.

Furthermore, economic inequality also plays a role in perpetuating the cycle of homelessness. Many individuals who are homeless face barriers to accessing stable housing, such as poor credit history or criminal records, which are often a result of economic hardship. Without access to affordable housing options, individuals who are experiencing homelessness are left with few options for finding stable housing, leading to a cycle of homelessness that is difficult to break. Economic inequality exacerbates this cycle by limiting opportunities for individuals to improve their financial situation and find stable housing.

Addressing economic inequality and housing affordability is crucial to addressing the issue of homelessness in America. By creating policies that promote economic equality and provide affordable housing options for low-income individuals and families, we can help to prevent homelessness and provide support for those who are experiencing housing instability. Additionally, investing in programs that provide resources and support for individuals who are homeless can help to break the cycle of homelessness and provide opportunities for individuals to regain stability in their lives.

It is essential that we work together as a society to address these issues and ensure that all Americans have access to safe and stable housing.

By addressing these issues through policy changes and increased support for affordable housing options, we can work towards ending the cycle of homelessness and providing opportunities for individuals to regain stability in their lives. It is crucial that we come together as a society to address these issues and ensure that all Americans have access to safe and stable housing.

Lack of Affordable Healthcare

In America, healthcare is a basic necessity that many people struggle to afford. For the homeless population in particular, access to affordable healthcare is even more challenging. Without a stable income or a permanent address, homeless individuals often face barriers to receiving medical care, leading to a lack of preventative care and treatment for chronic conditions.

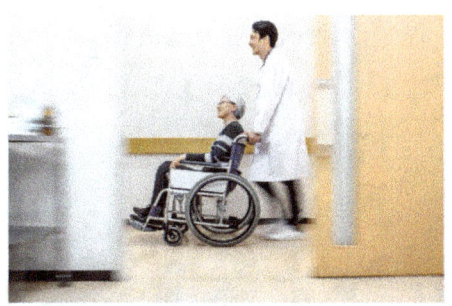

The cost of healthcare in America continues to rise, making it increasingly difficult for low-income individuals, including the homeless, to access essential medical services. Many homeless individuals rely on emergency rooms for their healthcare needs, which can be costly and ineffective in addressing long-term health issues. Without affordable healthcare options, homeless individuals are left vulnerable to untreated illnesses and injuries, putting their lives at risk.

The lack of affordable healthcare for the homeless population also contributes to the cycle of poverty and homelessness. Without access to preventative care and treatment for chronic conditions, homeless individuals are more likely to experience worsening health outcomes, leading to increased medical costs and barriers to finding stable housing and employment. The inability to afford healthcare further marginalizes the homeless population, perpetuating their struggles to escape poverty and homelessness.

As Americans, it is crucial to address the lack of affordable healthcare for the homeless population and work towards solutions that prioritize the health and well-being of all individuals. Investing in preventative care and community health resources can help reduce the burden on emergency rooms and improve health outcomes for homeless individuals. By advocating for policies that expand access to affordable healthcare, we can help break the cycle of poverty and homelessness for those most in need.

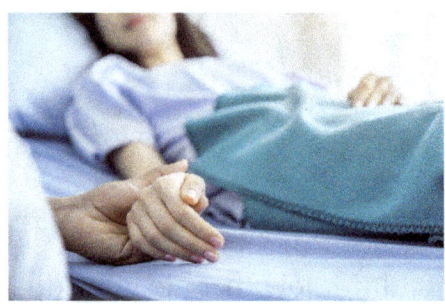

Together, we can ensure that all Americans, including the homeless population, have access to the healthcare they need to live healthy and fulfilling lives. By recognizing the challenges faced by homeless individuals in accessing affordable healthcare and working towards solutions that prioritize their well-being, we can create a more just and equitable society for all. Let us come together to address the issue of lack of affordable healthcare for the homeless and ensure that everyone has the opportunity to live a life of dignity and health.

Mental Illness and Substance Abuse

Mental illness and substance abuse are two interconnected issues that greatly impact the homeless population in America. Many individuals experiencing homelessness struggle with mental health disorders such as depression, anxiety, and PTSD. These conditions can make it difficult for them to maintain stable housing and employment, leading to a cycle of homelessness and despair. Additionally, substance abuse is a common coping mechanism for those dealing with mental illness, further exacerbating their struggles, and making it even harder to break free from homelessness.

The connection between mental illness and substance abuse among the homeless is complex and often misunderstood by the general public. Many people wrongly assume that individuals experiencing homelessness are solely responsible for their circumstances and that they could simply "pull themselves up by their bootstraps" if they wanted to. However, the reality is that mental illness and substance abuse are serious health issues that require proper treatment and support.

Unfortunately, the homeless population in America often lacks access to adequate mental health and addiction services. Many individuals living on the streets are unable to afford or access the necessary medications, therapy, and treatment programs they need to overcome their mental health challenges. This lack of support only serves to perpetuate the cycle of homelessness and substance abuse, leaving many individuals feeling trapped and hopeless.

As Americans, it is crucial that we recognize the connection between mental illness and substance abuse among the homeless and work towards providing better access to treatment and support services. By investing in mental health and addiction resources for the homeless population, we can help break the cycle of homelessness and improve the overall well-being of our communities. It is only by addressing the root causes of homelessness, including mental health and substance abuse, that we can truly make a difference in the lives of those who are struggling the most.

As a society, it is our responsibility to ensure that all individuals have the resources and support they need to overcome their mental health challenges and build a brighter future for themselves.

Hopeful Stories for the Homeless

The situations that homeless individuals face are both complex and multilayered. The factors often intersect and overlap, creating a web of challenges that individuals face. Homelessness is a complicated social issue, and addressing it effectively requires a comprehensive and compassionate approach that considers the unique circumstances of each person experiencing homelessness.

An anecdote from my son, who once worked for a recycling company, highlights the challenges faced by the homeless in Seattle. Upon arriving at a well-known restaurant, the recycling trucks were met by a group of homeless individuals eagerly awaiting its opening. Seeking assistance, some hoped to use the restroom, while others sought a meal. However, when the recycling truck entered the parking lot, the crowd would approach, attempting to beg the driver for money. Fearing for their safety, the truck driver would hastily leave the premises, prompting the restaurant owner to move the recycling bin to the curb. Consequently, the recycling company refused to enter the parking lot, fearing further encounters with the homeless.

It raises poignant questions: *why has over a billion dollars been allocated to Ukraine in a single year for defense, a country comparable in size to Texas, when a comparable amount has not been dedicated to alleviating homelessness among Americans?* Major cities like New York, Los Angeles, Chicago, San Francisco, and Seattle are grappling with an overwhelming number of people living on the streets. While I acknowledge the challenges faced by states like Texas, California, and Arizona due to an influx of immigrant populations, my heartfelt plea is directed at addressing the needs of homeless Americans – our mothers, fathers, sisters, brothers, aunts, uncles, and children. Let us open a dialogue about the circumstances leading to their homelessness and extend a helping hand to those in need.

I believe the primary catalyst for homelessness lies in substance abuse, a longstanding issue in the United States that the opioid crisis has exacerbated. Individuals seeking relief from pain initially sought assistance from doctors, unwittingly falling victim to the addictive nature of powerful painkillers such as Percocet and Oxycodone. As awareness grew about the addictive properties of Oxycodone, doctors abruptly ceased prescribing the drug, leaving those dependent on it without a structured process for withdrawal.

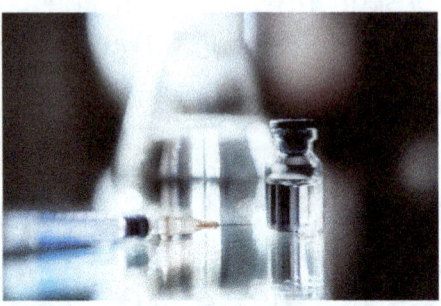

This abrupt cessation, akin to decelerating from 100 mph to 0 mph in 30 seconds, resulted in what can be described as pharmaceutical whiplash, pushing many to turn to heroin as a substitute painkiller. Unfortunately, society now tends to view these individuals as undesirable instead of addressing the root cause, which medical professionals initiated.

The crucial solution lies in rehabilitation for these addicts. However, some states, like New Jersey, refuse insurance coverage for rehab, leaving individuals facing insurmountable costs of around $15,000 for rehabilitation. I propose that rehabilitation costs should be covered by health insurance since addiction, a form of mental illness, was induced by the very doctors whose services were paid for by the individual's health insurance.

This prompts the question: *How have we stigmatized these individuals without holding accountable the doctors who prescribed these drugs?*

licensed drug dealers

Let's delve into the diverse causes of homelessness, examining the unique challenges faced by various groups: the individual grappling with addiction, the vulnerable sick and elderly, the disabled veteran coping with post-service difficulties, those contending with mental health issues, the convicted felon seeking societal reintegration, and the minimum wage worker navigating economic hardships.

3

FICTIONAL STORY: TERRY-THE LIFELONG ADDICT

Fictional Story: Terry-The Lifelong Addict

In the heart of the city, where the neon lights cast a dim glow on the cold pavement, lived Terry. She was a woman weathered by life's storms; a once vibrant soul reduced to the harsh reality of homelessness. The alleyways became her home, and the streets were her constant companion. Terry's days were spent navigating the concrete jungle, where survival often meant doing whatever it took to silence the gnawing hunger and numb the pain. She turned tricks under flickering streetlights, stole from unsuspecting victims, and manipulated those who showed a glimmer of kindness. The drugs provided a fleeting escape from the harshness of her existence, a momentary reprieve from the relentless struggles.

Yet, amid the chaos of her life, Terry harbored a flicker of hope, a distant dream that whispered of redemption and change. Deep within her hardened heart, she yearned for a chance to rebuild her shattered life, to break free from the shackles that bound her to the streets.

A kind stranger approached her one chilly night as Terry huddled beneath a tattered blanket. Samantha, a social worker dedicated to helping the homeless, saw beyond the layers of grime and despair. She recognized the pain etched on Terry's face and sensed the desperation that fueled her destructive choices.

With compassion in her eyes, Samantha spoke to Terry about a program that could provide her with a stable home and access to government assistance. Terry's initial resistance crumbled as she listened to the possibility of a different life where she wouldn't need to resort to tricks, theft, and manipulation to survive.

Overcoming skepticism, Terry took a leap of faith. With Samantha's guidance, she navigated the bureaucratic maze to secure a small, modest apartment. The four walls became a sanctuary, shielding her from the harsh elements and offering a chance for self-reflection.

As Terry settled into her new home, the support didn't end. Samantha connected her with counseling services, addiction treatment programs, and job placement initiatives. Slowly but surely, Terry began to rebuild her life. She confronted the demons that haunted her, faced the consequences of her past actions, and embraced the opportunity for change.

The path was challenging, marked by setbacks and moments of doubt, but Terry's resilience prevailed. She discovered strength within herself that she never knew existed. With the newfound stability of a home, she channeled her energy into rebuilding relationships, seeking employment, and overcoming addiction.

The story of Terry became a testament to the transformative power of compassion, support, and a chance at redemption. Through the kindness of others and her determination, Terry emerged from the shadows of her past, leaving behind a life of desperation and finding a way to contribute to society positively and meaningfully.

Fictional Story: Debbie, The Elderly & Sick

Debbie's life had become a series of harsh challenges, each hurdle seemingly higher than the last. The city she roamed had once been her home, but now the streets were all she knew. Her daily struggle for survival was exacerbated by debilitating respiratory issues that sent her to the hospital time and again.

The cycle was relentless, and Debbie's health continued to deteriorate. Each hospital stay offered temporary respite from the harsh realities of homelessness, but it was only a matter of time before she found herself back on the unforgiving streets.

Her dreams of finding a stable home were crushed by the weight of bad credit and history, which led to her being kicked off HUD assistance. The stigma of her past mistakes haunted every attempt to secure housing. Landlords turned her away, their doors closing like a fortress against her desperate pleas for shelter.

As her respiratory problems worsened, Debbie's resolve to change her life grew stronger. She knew that a stable environment was crucial for managing her health, yet the elusive goal of finding an affordable apartment remained just out of reach.

One day, fate intervened as she was sitting on a park bench, coughing into a tattered handkerchief. A compassionate outreach worker named Emily noticed Debbie's struggle and approached her with genuine concern. Emily had experience navigating the complex web of social services and was determined to help Debbie break free from the cycle of homelessness.

Emily learned about Debbie's past challenges with HUD assistance and bad credit. Undeterred, she began tirelessly advocating on Debbie's behalf. She sought out affordable housing options, reached out to landlords willing to give someone a second chance, and explored alternative avenues of support.

After numerous setbacks, Emily finally found a landlord willing to look beyond Debbie's credit history and provide her with an opportunity. It wasn't a luxurious apartment but a place to call home—a refuge from the streets that had taken a toll on Debbie's health.

With a roof over her head, Debbie's life began to change. Emily connected her with healthcare services to manage her respiratory issues and provided guidance on financial literacy to help rebuild her credit. Slowly, Debbie regained a sense of stability that had long eluded her.

The hospital visits became less frequent, replaced by visits to her new home. Debbie's determination and Emily's unwavering support allowed her to turn the page on a chapter marked by hardship and despair. As she settled into her modest apartment, Debbie found the strength to confront her health issues and forge a path toward a brighter future—one filled with hope and the promise of a better life.

Fictional Story: Joe- The Disabled Veteran

Joe's journey had taken him from the frontlines of the battlefield to the harsh realities of the streets. As a disabled veteran grappling with the invisible wounds of PTSD, his life had become a battlefield of its own. The echoes of war reverberated in his mind, and the nightmares that haunted his sleep led him to a dark path of drug abuse.

The shelters provided only temporary relief, a brief respite from the cold and unforgiving streets. The cycle of seeking refuge in shelters and succumbing to the numbing embrace of drugs became Joe's routine, a desperate attempt to drown out the memories that haunted him.

The bureaucratic maze of HUD assistance seemed insurmountable. Joe's name lingered on a waiting list, buried among countless others, each hoping for a chance at stable housing.

The reality of his drug abuse only exacerbated the situation, causing him to fall through the cracks of a system overwhelmed by the sheer magnitude of homelessness.

Amidst the despair, a glimmer of hope emerged in the form of a dedicated outreach worker named Lisa. Having witnessed the struggles of veterans like Joe before, she approached him with empathy rather than judgment. Lisa saw beyond the addiction, recognizing the hero beneath the scars of war.

Together, they embarked on a journey to break free from the cycle that bound Joe to the streets. Lisa connected him with rehabilitation services, helping him confront the demons that led to drug dependency. It was a tumultuous journey, filled with setbacks and relapses, but Joe's determination to overcome his addiction gradually gained strength.

While Joe battled his inner demons, Lisa tirelessly advocated on his behalf within the labyrinth of social services. She found a supportive housing program specifically designed for veterans, offering counseling and rehabilitation services tailored to their unique needs.

As Joe gradually weaned himself off drugs, the waiting list for HUD assistance became a bit more bearable. Lisa's tenacity paid off, and a small apartment in a veterans' housing complex became available. It wasn't just a place to live; it was a sanctuary where Joe could rebuild his life.

With a roof over his head and the support of fellow veterans, Joe began the slow process of healing. The scars of war may never fully fade, but he found solace in the camaraderie of those who understood his pain. Lisa continued to be a pillar of support, ensuring that Joe received the ongoing assistance he needed to maintain his newfound stability.

In this story of resilience, compassion, and second chances, Joe's journey from the streets to a stable home became a testament to the transformative power of understanding, support, and the unwavering belief that every veteran, no matter how lost, deserves a chance to reclaim their life.

Fictional Story: Phil-The Convicted Felon

Phil's life had been a tumultuous journey, marked by the shadows of addiction and the scars of incarceration. For over three decades, he had battled the demons that clung to him like a relentless storm. Despite carrying a Section 8 voucher, the beacon of hope for many in his situation, finding a stable place to call home remained an elusive dream.

His past, riddled with the consequences of addiction and a stint behind bars, cast a long and unforgiving shadow over his present. The Section 8 voucher, a lifeline for many, felt like an empty promise as Phil faced rejection after rejection from landlords unwilling to overlook his troubled history.

Phil's journey took an unexpected turn when he crossed paths with Sarah, a social worker with a heart for those societies often deemed irredeemable. Sarah saw beyond Phil's criminal record and credit history; she saw a person desperately seeking a chance at redemption.

Together, they navigated the complex web of housing applications and landlord meetings. Each rejection stung, but Sarah's unwavering support kept Phil from succumbing to despair. She connected him with credit counseling services, helping him take small but meaningful steps toward rebuilding his financial history.

The road to stability was paved with setbacks, but Phil's determination shone through. Sarah tirelessly advocated on his behalf, engaging in conversations with landlords, sharing stories of resilience, and emphasizing Phil's commitment to turning his life around.

One day, a breakthrough occurred. A compassionate landlord named Mr. Anderson saw past Phil's troubled past and decided to give him a chance. It wasn't a lavish apartment but a place to call home—a sanctuary where Phil could rebuild his life.

With a roof over his head, Phil continued to work on his recovery. Support groups became a cornerstone of his rehabilitation, providing a network of understanding and encouragement. Sarah remained a steadfast companion, ensuring Phil had access to the necessary resources for his journey toward stability.

As Phil settled into his new home, the electricity glowing warmly in the background, he reflected on the transformative power of compassion and second chances. The walls around him whispered stories of resilience, each crack and crevice a testament to the battles he had faced. Phil's journey from the shadows of addiction and incarceration to the embrace of a stable home became a beacon of hope for those who, like him, dared to believe in the possibility of redemption.

Fictional Story: Ashley-The Mentally Ill

Ashley's life had been a series of fragmented moments, her reality woven with threads of schizophrenia that often distorted the world around her. Her family, comprised of supportive brothers and sisters, had always tried to provide her with a semblance of stability. Yet, despite their efforts, finding a place to call her own proved to be an elusive dream.

Each sibling had, at different times, opened their doors to Ashley, offering her refuge from the turbulent storms that raged within her mind. However, her inability to trust others, a symptom of her mental illness, cast a shadow on the foundations of these living arrangements.

The cycle repeated: Ashley would move in with a sibling, and her struggles to maintain consistent payments soon clouded the initial promise of stability. Rent, a symbol of financial responsibility, became a labyrinth of confusion for her. When questioned, she would forget to pay and assert that she had already settled her debts. The pattern strained the bonds between Ashley and her siblings, testing their patience and understanding.

It wasn't that Ashley didn't want to contribute; her mental condition simply hindered her ability to manage routine responsibilities. The constant fluctuations in her perception of reality made it difficult for her to grasp the concept of financial commitments, leading to a breakdown in communication with her family.

Recognizing the need for a different approach, Ashley's family began to explore options for stable housing that catered to her unique needs. They connected with mental health professionals who specialized in supportive housing for individuals with schizophrenia. This type of housing provided not only shelter, but also on-site support services tailored to individuals facing mental health challenges.

Ashley found a haven in her new home designed to accommodate her condition. Support staff were trained to work with individuals experiencing schizophrenia, fostering an environment of understanding and patience. The structured routines of the supportive housing community helped Ashley manage her daily tasks, including paying rent, with the assistance of dedicated case managers.

Over time, Ashley's mental health stabilized in a supportive environment. The consistent care and encouragement she received allowed her to build trust with the staff and, gradually, with herself. As her world became more predictable, the financial aspects of stable housing became less daunting.

Ashley's siblings, relieved to see her in a place that nurtured her well-being, noticed a positive transformation. The stability of supportive housing not only provided Ashley with physical shelter but also became a catalyst for her mental and emotional healing.

In this story, Ashley's journey illustrates the profound impact of stable and supportive housing on individuals facing mental health challenges. It becomes a foundation for rebuilding trust, fostering personal growth, and creating a sense of security that contributes to overall well-being.

These narratives are crafted with positive resolutions, symbolizing the hope that these individuals might cross paths with someone able or willing to lift them from the hardships of homelessness. However, the harsh truth remains disheartening.

Fictional Story: Last but not least is Marcus-The Minimum Wage Worker.

Meet Marcus, a hardworking and resilient black man in his mid-50s who earns a minimum wage. Despite his dedication to his job, he finds himself grappling with the harsh reality of being unable to afford a place to live due to exorbitant rent increases.

With a warm smile reflecting his determination, Marcus works long hours in a job that barely covers his basic needs. He takes pride in his work, displaying a strong work ethic that has earned him respect among his colleagues. However, the rising cost of living, particularly the steep increases in rental prices, has left him in a precarious situation.

Marcus's face carries the weight of the challenges he faces daily. Despite his best efforts, the dream of having a stable and secure home seems out of reach. His evenings are often spent searching for affordable housing options, but the harsh reality of the inflated rental market makes the search daunting.

His situation highlights the broader societal issue of economic inequality, where hardworking individuals like Marcus find themselves on the fringes of stability. Despite facing these difficulties, Marcus remains hopeful, resilient, and committed to improving his circumstances. He represents the struggles of many individuals who are caught in the grip of economic challenges, emphasizing the need for solutions that address affordable housing and income inequality.

4

AVERAGE MINIMUM WAGE

As of January 2022, the federal minimum wage in the United States was $7.25 per hour. This rate was last increased in 2009. However, it's important to note that individual states can set their own minimum wage, which may be higher than the federal minimum. Additionally, some cities and local jurisdictions also have their own minimum wage rates.

There are exceptions to the federal minimum wage. For example, certain employees, such as those who receive tips, may have a lower minimum wage, known as the tipped minimum wage. The idea is that tips supplement their income. Employers are required to ensure that the combined total of tips and the lower hourly wage equals at least the federal minimum wage.

The Price Of Housing

These figures can vary significantly based on the specific location, urban or rural setting, and other factors. Additionally, housing prices can change over time due to various economic factors.

1 Bedroom Apartment:

National Average: The average rent for a 1-bedroom apartment can vary widely, but as a rough estimate, it might range from $1,200 to $1,800 per month, depending on the location.

2-Bedroom Apartment:

National Average: For a 2-bedroom apartment, the average rent might be in the range of $1,500 to $2,500 per month, again depending on the location.

3 Bedroom House:

National Average: Rent for a 3-bedroom house can vary significantly based on factors such as location and amenities. On average, it might range from $2,000 to $3,500 per month.

These figures are rough estimates, and the actual costs can be higher or lower depending on the city, state, and local housing market conditions. Additionally, if you are considering purchasing a house rather than renting, home prices will vary even more widely based on the factors mentioned above.

Let's look at a big desirable city like New York, NY.

Affording an apartment in New York City on a minimum wage income can be extremely challenging, as the cost of living, including housing, is generally high. The federal minimum wage is $7.25 per hour, but it's important to note that some states and cities, including New York, have set their own minimum wage rates, which can be higher. For example, in New York City, the minimum wage was higher than in other parts of the state.

As of 2023, the minimum wage in New York City was tiered based on employer size and other factors. Here is a general breakdown:
Large Employers (11 or more employees): $15.00 per hour
Small Employers (10 or fewer employees): $15.00 per hour

Living in a high-cost city like New York City, even with an hourly wage of $15, can still be challenging due to the high cost of living, particularly housing. However, here are some strategies that individuals earning $15 per hour might consider to make living in NYC more financially manageable:

Create a detailed budget to track income and expenses. Prioritize essential expenses such as rent, utilities, and groceries. Consider sharing living expenses by having roommates. Renting with others can significantly reduce individual housing costs. Explore affordable housing programs or initiatives offered by the city or state. Use public transportation instead of owning a car to save on commuting costs. Seek additional part-time or freelance work to supplement income.

Explore gig economy opportunities or side jobs. Check eligibility for government assistance programs that may provide financial support. Take advantage of discounts and savings on everyday expenses like food and entertainment. Save for emergencies to handle unexpected expenses without resorting to high-interest debt. Pursue opportunities for career advancement or additional training to increase earning potential over time. Consider living in neighborhoods with lower housing costs, even if they are outside the most central areas.

5

THE CHALLENGES FACED BY THE HOMELESS POPULATION

Access to Basic Needs

As Americans, we often take for granted the access we have to basic needs such as food, shelter, and healthcare. However, for the homeless population in America, these essential resources can be incredibly hard to come by. In this subchapter, we will explore the challenges that homeless individuals face when trying to access their basic needs, and the impact that lack of access can have on their lives.

One of the biggest obstacles that homeless individuals face when trying to access basic needs is the lack of affordable housing. With rising rent prices and a shortage of affordable housing options, many individuals find themselves living on the streets or in overcrowded shelters. This lack of stable housing can have a domino effect on a person's ability to access other basic needs, such as food and healthcare.

Access to nutritious food is another challenge that homeless individuals often face. Many are forced to rely on food pantries, soup kitchens, and shelters for their meals, which may not always provide the most nutritious options. This can lead to poor health outcomes and exacerbate existing medical conditions. Additionally, the stigma surrounding homelessness can make it difficult for individuals to access food assistance programs without facing discrimination or judgement.

Access to healthcare is another critical need that homeless individuals struggle to access. Without a stable address or insurance, many homeless individuals are unable to receive the medical care they need. This can lead to untreated medical conditions, mental health issues, and substance abuse problems. Lack of access to healthcare can also result in frequent emergency room visits, which are costly and unsustainable for both the individual and the healthcare system.

In order to address the issue of access to basic needs for the homeless population in America, it is essential that we as a society work together to create more affordable housing options, increase access to nutritious food, and expand healthcare services for those in need. By prioritizing the needs of our most vulnerable citizens, we can create a more equitable and compassionate society for all. It is imperative that we recognize the struggles that homeless individuals face in accessing their basic needs, and work towards solutions that will help alleviate their suffering and improve their quality of life.

Discrimination and Stigma

Discrimination and stigma are pervasive issues that the homeless population in America faces on a daily basis. Despite the fact that homelessness can affect anyone, regardless of their background or circumstances, many Americans hold negative stereotypes and prejudices against those who are experiencing homelessness. This discrimination can manifest in a variety of ways, from being denied access to housing and employment opportunities to facing verbal and physical abuse on the streets.

One of the most damaging aspects of discrimination and stigma against the homeless is the way it perpetuates a cycle of poverty and marginalization. When individuals are constantly faced with rejection and judgment from society, it can be incredibly difficult for them to break free from the cycle of homelessness. This creates a self-fulfilling prophecy in which the homeless are unable to access the resources and opportunities they need to improve their situation.

Furthermore, discrimination and stigma can have serious implications for the mental and emotional well-being of homeless individuals. Constantly being dehumanized and devalued by society can lead to feelings of despair, hopelessness, and worthlessness. This can exacerbate existing mental health issues and make it even more challenging for individuals to seek help and support.

It is essential for Americans to challenge their own biases and assumptions about homelessness in order to combat discrimination and stigma. By recognizing the humanity and dignity of every individual, regardless of their housing status, we can begin to create a more inclusive and compassionate society. This includes advocating for policies and initiatives that prioritize the needs and rights of the homeless

population, as well as supporting organizations and programs that provide essential resources and services to those in need.

Ultimately, addressing discrimination and stigma against the homeless is not only a matter of social justice, but also a necessary step towards creating a more equitable and caring society for all Americans. By working together to challenge stereotypes and promote empathy and understanding, we can begin to break down the barriers that keep individuals experiencing homelessness invisible and marginalized in America.

Limited Opportunities for Employment and Education

For many Americans, the ability to find stable employment and access to quality education is often taken for granted. However, for the homeless population in America, these opportunities are severely limited. Without a permanent address or access to basic necessities, finding a job or enrolling in school can seem like an impossible task.

One of the biggest challenges facing the homeless population is the lack of resources and support systems available to help them secure employment. Many homeless individuals struggle with mental health issues, substance abuse, or physical disabilities that can make it difficult for them to hold down a job. Without access to proper medical care or treatment, these barriers can become insurmountable obstacles to finding gainful employment.

In addition to the challenges of securing employment, homeless individuals also face significant barriers to accessing education. Without a stable living situation, it can be nearly impossible for homeless students to attend school regularly or complete their coursework. The lack of access to technology, textbooks, and other necessary resources further hinders their ability to succeed academically.

Furthermore, the stigma and discrimination that homeless individuals face can also impact their ability to find employment or pursue education. Many employers and educational institutions may be hesitant to hire or admit someone who is homeless, viewing them as unreliable or a potential liability. This perpetuates a cycle of poverty and homelessness, further limiting their opportunities for success.

In order to address these challenges, it is crucial for Americans to advocate for policies and programs that provide support and resources to the homeless population. By investing in affordable housing, mental health services, job training programs, and educational opportunities, we can help break the cycle of homelessness and provide a pathway

to a brighter future for those in need. It is only through collective action and compassion that we can ensure that all Americans have the opportunity to thrive, regardless of their housing status.

6

OVERCOMING HOMELESSNESS IN AMERICA

Overcoming homelessness is a challenging process that often requires a multi-faceted approach. Here are resources that homeless individuals can consider securing stable housing:

- Contact local shelters or emergency housing services to find immediate shelter. Many communities have shelters offering temporary stays, meals, and basic amenities.
- Seek assistance from outreach programs and social service agencies. Outreach workers can provide information on available resources, including shelters, food programs, and healthcare services.
- Explore supportive housing programs designed to assist individuals facing homelessness, especially those with specific needs such as mental health issues or substance abuse. These programs often provide not only housing but also supportive services.

- Investigate government assistance programs, such as Housing and Urban Development (HUD) programs, Section 8 vouchers, or other subsidized housing options. Local social service agencies can provide information and help with the application process.
- Look for employment opportunities to generate income. Local job placement agencies, career centers, and community organizations may offer support in job searches and skill development.
- Connect with mental health services and substance abuse treatment programs to address underlying issues. Many communities have clinics or organizations that offer support and counseling.
- Cultivate relationships with friends, family, or support groups. Having a support system can provide emotional encouragement and practical assistance in the journey toward stable housing.
- Transitional housing programs provide short- to medium-term housing with the goal of helping individuals transition to permanent housing. These programs often offer supportive services and assistance in building life skills.
- Address any credit issues that may be hindering housing opportunities. Nonprofit organizations and credit counseling services can provide guidance on repairing credit.
- Participate in workshops or training programs that focus on financial literacy, job skills, and other practical skills that can enhance employability and self-sufficiency.
- Seek legal assistance if facing legal barriers, such as eviction records or criminal histories that may affect housing options. Legal aid organizations may be able to provide guidance.
- Transitional services, including case management, can provide ongoing support as individuals work towards

stable housing. These services may help navigate challenges and connect individuals with necessary resources.

7

THE ROLE OF GOVERNMENT AND NONPROFIT ORGANIZATIONS

Government Programs and Policies

Government Programs and Policies play a crucial role in addressing the issue of homelessness in America. These programs are designed to provide support and resources to individuals who are experiencing homelessness, with the goal of helping them secure stable housing and improve their overall well-being. However, the effectiveness of these programs can vary greatly, and many homeless individuals still struggle to access the services they need.

One of the most well-known government programs aimed at addressing homelessness is the Housing First approach. This approach prioritizes providing individuals with stable housing as quickly as possible, with the belief that having a safe and secure place to live is essential for addressing other challenges such as mental health issues and substance abuse. While Housing First has shown promising results in reducing homelessness in some communities, there are still many barriers that prevent homeless individuals from accessing this program.

In addition to Housing First, there are a variety of other government programs and policies that aim to address homelessness in America. These include emergency shelters, transitional housing programs, and supportive services such as job training and mental health counseling. However, many homeless individuals face challenges in accessing these programs, such as long waitlists, lack of transportation, and limited funding for services.

Furthermore, government policies such as cuts to social services and affordable housing programs can exacerbate the issue of homelessness in America. When funding for programs that support homeless individuals is reduced, it becomes even more difficult for them to access the resources they need to secure stable housing and improve their lives. Advocates for the homeless continue to push for increased funding and support for these programs, in order to ensure that all individuals have the opportunity to escape homelessness and build a better future for themselves.

Homeless Shelters and Support Services

In America, the issue of homelessness is a harsh reality that many individuals face on a daily basis. Homeless shelters and

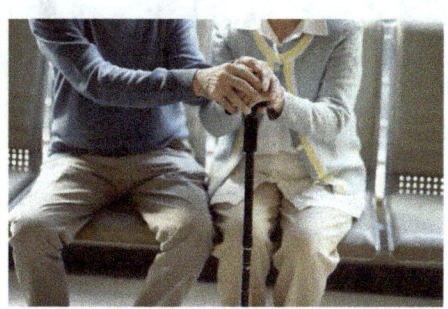

support services play a crucial role in providing a safe haven for those without a place to call home. These shelters offer temporary housing, meals, and resources to help individuals get back on their feet.

Homeless shelters are often the first line of defense for individuals experiencing homelessness. These shelters provide a warm bed, a hot meal, and a safe place to rest for those who have nowhere else to go. They offer a sense of security and stability in an otherwise chaotic world. Support services within these shelters also provide individuals with access to resources such as job training, mental health services, and substance abuse treatment.

Despite the important role that homeless shelters play in our society, they are often underfunded and over capacity. Many shelters struggle to meet the growing demand for their services, leaving many individuals without a place to turn. This lack of resources can have devastating consequences for those experiencing homelessness, leading to increased rates of mental illness, substance abuse, and chronic health conditions.

As Americans, it is our responsibility to support and advocate for homeless shelters and support services in our communities. By volunteering our time, donating resources, and advocating for increased funding, we can help ensure that these vital services continue to provide a lifeline for those in need. Together, we can make a difference in the lives of the homeless individuals in America.

Advocacy and Outreach Efforts

Advocacy and Outreach Efforts play a crucial role in addressing the issue of homelessness in America. Various organizations and individuals are working tirelessly to advocate for the rights and needs of the homeless population. These efforts aim to raise awareness about the challenges faced by the homeless and to push for policy changes that can help improve their situation. By engaging in advocacy and outreach efforts, we can make a real difference in the lives of those who are invisible in our society.

One of the key goals of advocacy and outreach efforts is to ensure that the voices of the homeless are heard. Many homeless individuals face stigma and discrimination, which can make it difficult for them to speak up about their needs and experiences. Advocates work to amplify these voices, providing a platform for the homeless to share their stories and advocate for the resources and support they need to thrive. By centering the voices of the homeless in advocacy efforts, we can work towards creating a more inclusive and compassionate society.

In addition to amplifying the voices of the homeless, advocacy and outreach efforts also focus on raising awareness about the root causes of homelessness. Many people are unaware of the systemic issues that contribute to homelessness, such as lack of affordable housing, poverty, and mental health challenges. By educating the public about these issues, advocates hope to shift perceptions and build support for solutions that address the underlying causes of homelessness. Through outreach efforts, we can foster empathy and understanding for the homeless population, helping to break down barriers and build a more compassionate society.

Advocacy and outreach efforts also play a crucial role in pushing for policy changes that can improve the lives of the homeless. Advocates work with lawmakers and policymakers to advocate for increased funding for affordable housing, mental health services, and other resources that can help prevent and address homelessness. By mobilizing support

and pushing for legislative changes, advocates can help create a more supportive environment for the homeless population. Through sustained advocacy efforts, we can work towards creating a society where everyone has access to safe and stable housing.

Advocacy and outreach efforts are essential in addressing the issue of homelessness in America. By amplifying the voices of the homeless, raising awareness about the root causes of homelessness, and pushing for policy changes, advocates are working towards creating a more inclusive and compassionate society.

As Americans, we all have a role to play in advocating for the rights and needs of the homeless population.By coming together and working towards solutions, we can make a real difference in the lives of those who are too often invisible in our society.

8

HOW MANY PEOPLE ARE HOMELESS IN AMERICA?

While it's challenging to provide real-time data, homelessness is a complex and dynamic issue, and the number of homeless individuals can change over time due to various factors.

As of 2020, before the COVID-19 pandemic, there were approximately 580,000 people experiencing homelessness in the United States, according to the Annual Homeless Assessment Report to Congress by the U.S. Department of Housing and Urban Development (HUD). Keep in mind that this figure is an estimate, and the actual number may fluctuate based on economic conditions, housing policies, and other factors.

There are twice that number of homeless Americans following the pandemic since many poor people failed to pay their portion of the rent during the 2-year moratorium on evictions.

One such personal case is my niece Tasha, who was responsible to pay $75 per month for her portion of her $850 rent. The remainder was paid through HUD assistance. Once the moratorium expired, Tasha owed her landlord $1800. Unable to pay, she was evicted. Not only did Tasha lose her cheap housing, but she ruined her credit by failing to pay her portion of the rent.

Additionally, Tasha was kicked off HUD for failing to pay her portion. In New Jersey, the waiting list for HUD is a three-year wait. Tasha will not likely be approved for HUD again; these days, she couch-surfs in friends' and relative's homes. Quite frankly, she has worn out her welcome everywhere.

For the most recent and accurate information on homelessness in the United States, check the latest reports from reputable sources such as HUD, the National Alliance to End Homelessness (NAEH), or other relevant government agencies and organizations.

Homelessness in America is a complex issue with multiple contributing factors. It often results from a combination of individual, economic, and systemic factors. While each person's situation is unique, some common reasons for homelessness in America include many factors such as affordable housing, economic factors, job loss, mental health, substance abuse and other reasons.

Rising housing costs in many urban areas make it difficult for low-income individuals and families to secure stable housing. Economic factors, such as poverty and low wages, play a significant role in homelessness. Individuals and families with limited financial resources may struggle to cover basic living expenses, including housing costs.

Job loss or the inability to secure stable employment can lead to financial instability and homelessness. Economic downturns, lack of job opportunities, and changes in industries can contribute to unemployment.

Individuals with mental health challenges may face difficulties in maintaining stable housing. Stigma, limited access to mental health services, and the high cost of treatment can exacerbate these challenges.

As stated earlier, substance abuse issues can contribute to homelessness, as addiction can strain relationships, employment, and housing stability. Homelessness, in turn, can further exacerbate substance abuse problems.

Survivors of domestic violence may become homeless as they escape abusive relationships. The lack of safe and affordable housing options can make it challenging for individuals and families to leave abusive situations.

Systemic racism contributes to disparities in income, education, and employment opportunities, affecting communities of color. This can result in higher rates of homelessness among minority populations.

Individuals released from correctional facilities, mental health institutions, or foster care systems may struggle to find stable housing upon reentry into society, contributing to homelessness.

Natural disasters, such as hurricanes, floods, or wildfires, can displace individuals and families, leading to homelessness. Recovery efforts may be slow, hindering the rebuilding of homes and communities. Family conflicts, breakdowns, or disputes can result in individuals, especially youth, leaving home and becoming homeless. This can be compounded by strained relationships or a lack of support networks.

Addressing homelessness requires comprehensive strategies that encompass affordable housing initiatives, mental health services, employment opportunities, and support for individuals and families facing various challenges. Government agencies, nonprofit organizations, and community initiatives play crucial roles in addressing the root causes of homelessness and providing assistance to those in need.

California has consistently had one of the highest homeless populations among U.S. states. Homelessness is a complex issue affected by various factors, including housing costs, economic conditions, and social services availability.

Cities like Los Angeles, San Francisco, and other major urban centers in California have faced significant challenges related to homelessness. However, homelessness is an issue that can change over time, and specific numbers may have shifted since the date of this book.

For the most current and accurate information on homelessness by state, it is recommended to refer to the latest reports and data provided by government agencies such as the U.S. Department of Housing and Urban Development (HUD) or reputable organizations focused on homelessness, like the National Alliance to End Homelessness (NAE).

9

PERSONAL STORIES OF STRUGGLE AND RESILIENCE

Overcoming Adversity

In America, the homeless population faces numerous challenges on a daily basis. From lack of access to basic necessities such as food and shelter, to discrimination and stigma from society, the adversity they face can seem insurmountable. However, despite these obstacles, many homeless individuals have shown incredible resilience and strength in overcoming their circumstances.

One common theme among those who have overcome homelessness is the importance of seeking help and support. Whether it be from social service agencies, shelters, or community organizations, reaching out for assistance can make a world of difference in getting back on one's feet. By connecting with resources that can provide housing, job training, and mental health support, individuals experiencing homelessness can take the first steps towards rebuilding their lives.

Another key factor in overcoming adversity for the homeless is maintaining a positive mindset. It can be easy to feel defeated and hopeless when faced with the challenges of homelessness, but staying optimistic and focused on the goal of finding stability can help individuals persevere through difficult times. By setting small, achievable goals and celebrating successes along the way, homeless individuals can build momentum towards a brighter future.

Additionally, building a support network of friends, family, and mentors can provide the encouragement and guidance needed to overcome adversity. Having a strong support system can offer emotional support, practical advice, and a sense of belonging that can help individuals facing homelessness feel less isolated and more empowered to make positive changes in their lives. By surrounding themselves with positive influences, homeless individuals can increase their chances of successfully overcoming adversity.

Ultimately, overcoming homelessness and the adversity that comes with it is a journey that requires determination, resilience, and a willingness to seek help. By taking small steps towards stability, maintaining a positive mindset, and building a strong support network, homeless individuals can overcome the challenges they face and create a brighter future for themselves. As Americans, it is important for us to recognize the strength and resilience of the homeless population and support efforts to provide them with the resources and opportunities they need to overcome adversity and thrive.

Finding Hope and Support

In the face of adversity, finding hope and support can be a lifeline for those experiencing homelessness in America. The journey of being homeless can be isolating and overwhelming, but it is important to remember that there are resources and individuals who are willing to offer assistance and guidance. By seeking out these sources of support, individuals can begin to rebuild their lives and work towards a brighter future.

One of the first steps in finding hope and support is reaching out to local shelters and organizations that specialize in assisting the homeless population. These organizations often provide essential services such as meals, shelter, and access to healthcare. Additionally, they may offer counseling and assistance with finding housing and employment opportunities. By connecting with these resources, individuals can begin to address their immediate needs and gain the support necessary to move forward.

Another valuable source of support for those experiencing homelessness is through community outreach programs and religious organizations. These groups often provide a sense of community and belonging, which can be crucial for individuals who may feel isolated or forgotten. By becoming involved in these programs, individuals can build relationships with others who understand their struggles and can offer encouragement and support along the way.

In addition to seeking out formal sources of support, it is also important for individuals experiencing homelessness to reach out to friends, family members, and other loved ones for assistance. Building a strong support network of people who care about their well-being can provide individuals with a sense of hope and encouragement during difficult times. By opening up about their struggles and asking for help when needed, individuals can begin to cultivate a sense of resilience and determination to overcome their challenges.

Ultimately, finding hope and support is a critical aspect of navigating the complexities of homelessness in America. By connecting with resources, community programs, and loved ones, individuals can begin to rebuild their lives and work towards a brighter future. It is important for all Americans to recognize the struggles faced by the homeless population and to offer support and compassion to those in need. Together, we can create a more inclusive and supportive society for all individuals experiencing homelessness in America.

Building a Path to Stability

In the United States, homelessness is a pervasive issue that affects millions of individuals and families. The homeless population is often overlooked and marginalized, struggling to find stable housing and access to basic necessities. In order to address this crisis, it is crucial for Americans to come together and build a path to stability for those who are experiencing homelessness.

One key aspect of creating a path to stability for the homeless is providing access to affordable housing. Many individuals and families who are homeless simply cannot afford a place to live, leading to a cycle of poverty and instability. By investing in affordable housing initiatives and programs, we can help provide a safe and secure place for those who are experiencing homelessness to rebuild their lives.

In addition to affordable housing, it is important to address the underlying causes of homelessness, such as mental illness, substance abuse, and lack of access to healthcare. By investing in mental health and substance abuse treatment programs, as well as increasing access to healthcare services, we can help individuals who are homeless address these issues and work towards stability.

Another crucial component of building a path to stability for the homeless is providing access to education and job training programs. Many individuals who are homeless face barriers to finding stable employment due to lack of education or job skills. By investing in education and job training programs, we can help individuals who are homeless gain the skills and knowledge they need to secure stable and sustainable employment.

Ultimately, building a path to stability for the homeless requires a collective effort from all Americans. By coming together to invest in affordable housing, mental health and substance abuse treatment programs, and education and job training initiatives, we can help individuals and families who are experiencing homelessness rebuild their lives and create a brighter future for themselves. It is time for us to recognize the humanity and dignity of those who are homeless and work together to ensure that everyone has a place to call home.

What do people report as their reason for being homeless?

People experiencing homelessness may cite various reasons for their circumstances, and these reasons are often multi-faceted and interconnected.

Many individuals and families struggle with the high cost of housing, especially in urban areas where housing prices are soaring. The shortage of affordable housing options contributes to homelessness.

Job loss or the inability to secure stable employment can lead to financial instability, making it challenging for people to afford housing. Living in poverty or earning low wages can make it difficult for individuals and families to cover basic living expenses, including rent and utilities.

Mental health issues, such as depression, anxiety, and other conditions, can interfere with an individual's ability to maintain stable housing. Stigma, lack of access to mental health services, and the high cost of treatment may contribute to homelessness. Substance abuse problems can lead to strained relationships, loss of employment, and housing instability. Homelessness, in turn, can exacerbate substance abuse issues.

Survivors of domestic violence may become homeless as they escape abusive relationships. The lack of safe and affordable housing options can pose a significant barrier to leaving abusive situations. Conflict, disputes, or breakdowns within families can result in individuals, particularly youth, leaving home and becoming homeless. Lack of support networks can contribute to housing instability.

Individuals released from correctional facilities, mental health institutions, or foster care systems may face challenges in finding stable housing upon reentry into society, contributing to homelessness.

Natural disasters, such as hurricanes, floods, or wildfires, can displace individuals and families, leading to homelessness. Slow recovery efforts may hinder the rebuilding of homes and communities.

Systemic issues such as racism, discrimination, and inequality can contribute to disparities in income, education, and employment opportunities, leading to higher rates of homelessness among marginalized communities.

The issue of homelessness needs to be addressed with empathy and recognized as a diverse and complicated issue. Many factors contribute to individuals' experiences of housing instability. Addressing homelessness requires comprehensive strategies that encompass affordable housing initiatives, Mental health and substance abuse services, employment opportunities, and social support networks.

10

HOUSING FIRST APPROACHES

Housing First approaches have gained popularity in recent years as a solution to the growing homelessness crisis in America. This strategy prioritizes providing stable, permanent housing for individuals experiencing homelessness before addressing any other issues they may be facing. The idea is that without a safe and stable place to live, it is nearly impossible for individuals to address other challenges they may be facing, such as mental health issues or substance abuse.

One of the key benefits of Housing First approaches is that they have been proven to be effective in reducing homelessness and improving the overall well-being of individuals experiencing homelessness. Studies have shown that providing individuals with stable housing first significantly reduces their use of emergency services, such as hospitals and jails, ultimately saving taxpayers money in the long run. By addressing the root cause of homelessness – the lack of affordable housing – Housing First approaches offer a more sustainable solution than temporary shelters or transitional housing programs.

Another important aspect of Housing First approaches is their emphasis on providing support services to help individuals maintain their housing stability. These services may include case management, mental health counseling, substance abuse treatment, and job training. By providing these wraparound services, individuals are better equipped to address the underlying issues that may have contributed to their homelessness in the first place. This holistic approach has been shown to be more effective in helping individuals achieve long-term housing stability and independence.

Despite the proven success of Housing First approaches, there are still challenges to implementing this strategy on a larger scale. One of the main obstacles is the lack of affordable housing options in many communities across America. Without an adequate supply of affordable housing, it is difficult to provide stable housing for individuals experiencing homelessness. Additionally, there may be resistance from some community members who are concerned about the potential impact of housing individuals experiencing homelessness in their neighborhoods.

Overall, Housing First approaches represent a promising solution to the homelessness crisis in America. By prioritizing stable, permanent housing for individuals experiencing homelessness and providing the necessary support services to help them maintain their housing stability, we can make significant strides in ending homelessness once and for all. It is crucial for policymakers, community leaders, and individuals alike to support and advocate for Housing First approaches in order to create a more just and equitable society for all Americans, including those who are currently experiencing homelessness.

Mental Health and Addiction Treatment

Mental health and addiction treatment are critical components of addressing the issues faced by the homeless population in America. Many individuals experiencing homelessness also struggle with mental health disorders such as depression, anxiety, and PTSD. Without access to proper treatment, these individuals may turn to self-medication through substance abuse, further exacerbating their mental health issues.

Unfortunately, the stigma surrounding mental health and addiction in America often prevents homeless individuals from seeking the help they need. Many are hesitant to admit they are struggling or fear judgment from others. This lack of access to treatment only perpetuates the cycle of homelessness and mental health issues.

It is essential for Americans to recognize the intersectionality of mental health and addiction within the homeless population. By addressing these underlying issues, we can begin to break down barriers to treatment and provide individuals with the support they need to rebuild their lives. This may involve increasing funding for mental health services and addiction treatment programs, as well as implementing more comprehensive care plans for those experiencing homelessness.

Additionally, education and awareness are key components of addressing mental health and addiction within the homeless community. By destigmatizing these issues and providing resources for those in need, we can create a more supportive environment for individuals to seek help and begin their journey towards recovery.

Overall, mental health and addiction treatment are essential aspects of addressing the struggles faced by the homeless population in America. By prioritizing these services and breaking down barriers to access, we can empower individuals to take control of their mental health and work towards a brighter future.

Community Support and Empowerment

In America, the struggle of the homeless is a pressing issue that affects millions of individuals every day. Despite the challenges they face, many homeless individuals find solace in the support and empowerment provided by their communities. Community support is essential in helping homeless individuals regain their sense of dignity and self-worth.

One way communities can support the homeless is by providing access to resources such as shelters, food banks, and medical care. These resources can make a significant difference in the lives of homeless individuals, helping them meet their basic needs and improve their quality of life. By coming together to provide these essential services, communities can help empower homeless individuals to take steps towards rebuilding their lives.

In addition to providing resources, communities can also offer emotional support to homeless individuals. Many homeless individuals face stigma and discrimination on a daily basis, which can take a toll on their mental health. By offering a listening ear, a kind word, or a helping hand, community members can help homeless individuals feel valued and supported.

Empowerment is another key aspect of community support for the homeless. By empowering homeless individuals to take control of their own lives, communities can help them break the cycle of homelessness and poverty. This can be done through education, job training programs, and other initiatives that help homeless individuals develop the skills and confidence they need to succeed.

Ultimately, community support and empowerment are crucial in addressing the issue of homelessness in America. By coming together to provide resources, emotional support, and opportunities for empowerment, communities can help homeless individuals rebuild their lives and regain their sense of dignity and self-worth. Together, we can make a difference in the lives of the homeless and create a more compassionate and inclusive society for all.

What race of people comprises the majority of the homeless?

Homelessness affects individuals from various racial and ethnic backgrounds, and the demographics of the homeless population can vary based on geographic location and other factors. However, certain racial and ethnic groups are often overrepresented among the homeless population in the United States.

African Americans have been disproportionately represented among the homeless population. Systemic factors, including historical and contemporary racial inequalities, contribute to this disparity. Native Americans also experience higher rates of homelessness compared to their percentage in the general population. Historical trauma, discrimination, and economic disparities are contributing factors. In some regions, the Latinx population faces increased homelessness, often linked to factors such as poverty, limited access to affordable housing, and immigration-related challenges.

Homelessness is a complex issue influenced by a range of factors, including systemic inequalities, economic conditions, and access to resources. Homelessness is not solely determined by race or ethnicity, but racial and ethnic minorities may face additional challenges and disparities that contribute to their higher representation in the homeless population.

Several factors contribute to an individual's or family's likelihood of experiencing homelessness. Again, homelessness is a complex issue influenced by a combination of individual, economic, and systemic factors. While anyone can face housing instability, certain groups are often more vulnerable. **Common risk factors include:**

Individuals and families who live in areas with high housing costs or experience a shortage of affordable housing options are more vulnerable to homelessness. People living in poverty or earning low wages may struggle to cover basic living expenses, including housing costs. Economic instability increases the risk of homelessness.

Job loss or the inability to secure stable employment can lead to financial instability, making it difficult for individuals to afford housing. Individuals with mental health issues may face difficulties maintaining stable housing. The stigma associated with mental health, lack of access to treatment, and the cost of care contribute to housing instability.

Substance abuse problems can strain relationships, lead to job loss, and contribute to housing instability. Individuals facing addiction may be at a higher risk of homelessness. Survivors of domestic violence may become homeless as they flee abusive relationships. The lack of safe and affordable housing options can present barriers to leaving abusive situations.

Systemic issues such as racism, discrimination, and inequality contribute to disparities in income, education, and employment opportunities, placing certain groups at higher risk of homelessness. Youth who age out of the foster care system may face challenges transitioning to independent living, increasing their risk of homelessness.

Individuals released from correctional facilities may encounter difficulties securing stable housing upon reentry into society, contributing to homelessness. People without strong social support networks or family resources may face increased challenges in times of crisis, making them more susceptible to homelessness.

11

TAKING ACTION AS INDIVIDUALS AND COMMUNITIES

Volunteering and Donating

As Americans, we are fortunate to live in a country that prides itself on generosity and compassion. Volunteering and donating are two powerful ways in which we can make a positive impact on the lives of those less fortunate, particularly the homeless population in America. By giving our time, resources, and support to those in need, we can help to alleviate suffering and create a more just and equitable society for all.

Volunteering is a vital way in which individuals can directly engage with and support the homeless community. Whether it be serving meals at a local shelter, organizing donation drives, or providing mentorship and support to homeless individuals, volunteering allows us to make a tangible difference in the lives of those who are struggling. By offering our time and skills, we can build relationships, foster empathy, and create a sense of community that is essential to helping individuals experiencing homelessness regain stability and dignity.

In addition to volunteering, donating is another crucial way in which we can support the homeless population in America. By giving financial contributions, clothing, food, and other essential items to organizations that work with the homeless, we can help to ensure that individuals have access to the resources they need to survive and thrive. Donating is a simple yet powerful way to make a difference, and every dollar or item given can have a meaningful impact on the lives of those in need.

It is important for all Americans to recognize that homelessness is a complex issue that requires a multifaceted approach to address. By volunteering and donating, we can play a part in addressing the root causes of homelessness, such as lack of affordable housing, economic inequality, and systemic discrimination. Through our collective efforts, we can advocate for policies that support and empower homeless individuals, while also working to create a more compassionate and inclusive society for all.

Advocacy and Policy Change

Advocacy and policy change are crucial components in addressing the issue of homelessness in America. While providing immediate assistance such as shelters and food are important, advocating for systemic changes is essential to create long-term solutions. Homeless individuals are often marginalized and overlooked in society, making it crucial for advocates to speak up on their behalf and push for policy changes that address the root causes of homelessness.

One of the key aspects of advocacy is raising awareness about the challenges faced by the homeless population. Many Americans are unaware of the complexities of homelessness and the numerous factors that contribute to someone becoming homeless. By educating the public about these issues, advocates can create a sense of empathy and understanding, leading to increased support for policies that address homelessness.

Advocates also play a vital role in pushing for policy changes at the local, state, and federal levels. This can include advocating for increased funding for affordable housing, mental health services, and job training programs. By working with lawmakers and policymakers, advocates can help shape legislation that addresses the root causes of homelessness and provides sustainable solutions for those experiencing homelessness.

In addition to advocating for policy changes, advocates also work to empower homeless individuals to become their own advocates. By providing resources and support, advocates can help homeless individuals navigate the complex systems that often perpetuate their homelessness. This can include helping individuals access social services, find stable housing, and secure employment.

Ultimately, advocacy and policy change are essential components in the fight against homelessness in America. By raising awareness, advocating for policy changes, and empowering homeless individuals, advocates can work towards creating a society where everyone has access to safe and stable housing. Together, we can make a difference in the lives of the homeless population and create a more equitable society for all Americans.

Creating a More Inclusive Society

Creating a more inclusive society is crucial in addressing the issue of homelessness in America. Homelessness affects individuals from all walks of life, and it is important for us as a society to come together and support those in need. By prioritizing inclusivity and understanding, we can work towards creating a more compassionate and supportive environment for those experiencing homelessness.

One way to create a more inclusive society is to challenge stereotypes and stigma surrounding homelessness. Many individuals experiencing homelessness face discrimination and judgment from others, which only serves to further isolate them from society. By educating ourselves and others about the realities of homelessness, we can work towards breaking down these harmful stereotypes and promoting empathy and understanding.

In addition to challenging stereotypes, it is important for us to actively listen to the voices of those experiencing homelessness. By centering their experiences and perspectives, we can gain a better understanding of the challenges they face and work towards finding solutions that are truly impactful. Creating spaces for individuals experiencing homelessness to share their stories and advocate for themselves is essential in building a more inclusive society.

Another important aspect of creating a more inclusive society is to prioritize access to resources and support for those experiencing homelessness. This includes access to affordable housing, mental health services, and employment opportunities. By investing in these resources and working towards policies that prioritize the needs of the homeless population, we can create a more equitable society that supports the well-being of all its members.

Ultimately, creating a more inclusive society is a collective effort that requires the participation and support of all Americans. By coming together to challenge stereotypes, listen to the voices of those experiencing homelessness, and prioritize access to resources, we can work towards building a society that is truly inclusive and supportive of all its members. It is only through this collective effort that we can truly address the issue of homelessness in America and create a more compassionate and just society for all.

Fictional Stories

Kevin, Dorothy, Zen and Dorlita Community Builders

In the heart of New York City, in a weather-beaten two-bedroom apartment, Kevin, a black man in his 30s, Dorothy, a white woman in her 20s, Zen, a Japanese managed 42, and Dorlita, a Hispanic woman aged 45, found solace in each other's company. Homeless but resilient, they had formed an unconventional family, sharing the struggles of life on the streets.

United by a common dream, the four friends decided to create their makeshift community. Calling themselves "Can Housing," they collected recyclable cans, turning discarded items into lifelines. Their ambition was grand – to change laws and open a homeless shelter to benefit others like them.

One day, as they scoured the city streets for cans, Kevin's life took an unexpected turn. Bending into a trash can, he lost his balance and fell right in front of Tee, a renowned figure accompanied by imposing bodyguards. The bodyguards threatened Kevin by misinterpreting the situation, but Tee intervened, recognizing the genuine accident. A connection sparked between them.

Feeling a sense of validation, Kevin asked for an autograph, to which Tee responded with four concert tickets and a backstage pass. Ecstatic, Kevin invited his friends to join him at the concert. The Can Housing crew arrived in a self-painted, 20-year-old car proudly displaying their business name. The car was a symbol of their resilience and determination.

When Tee took the stage, fans surged forward, attempting to storm it. Overwhelmed, Tee retreated to his dressing room, and in the hallway, he presented Kevin with a personal business card. Intrigued by their story, Tee agreed to a meeting to discuss their vision for affordable housing in New York City.

As the Can Housing crew navigated the world of business dealings, they faced numerous challenges. From securing funding to battling bureaucratic obstacles, the road was tough. Yet, the bonds they formed during their time on the streets became their foundation. Kevin's optimism, Dorothy's resourcefulness, Zen's wisdom, and Dorlita's resilience complemented each other, creating a formidable team.

Their meetings with Tee turned into a partnership, and together, they worked towards their goal. Through shared struggles and triumphs, the Can Housing crew not only transformed their lives but also the lives of many others.

In the end, their dream became a reality. With Tee's support and their unwavering determination, they opened a homeless shelter in the heart of New York City. The shelter, adorned with a mural depicting their journey, stood as a testament to the power of unity and shared dreams.

As they cut the ribbon on the shelter, Kevin, Dorothy, Zen, and Dorlita looked at each other with tears in their eyes. Their makeshift community had evolved into something extraordinary, proving that compassion, determination, and friendship could change the world despite adversity.

Billy, uncovers corruption

In the shadows of a sprawling metropolis, where the glittering skyline cast long and ominous shadows, Billy, a weathered and streetwise homeless man, found himself entangled in a web of mystery and corruption. The cold concrete streets of the city were his home, and his survival instincts were his only companions.

One chilly night, as Billy sought refuge in an abandoned warehouse, he overheard a hushed conversation between two men in tailored suits. The words "displace the undesirables" and "gentrification" caught his attention. Intrigued and wary, Billy decided to dig deeper into this cryptic conversation.

With nothing but a tattered backpack and a keen sense of survival, Billy began to unravel the threads of a conspiracy that went far beyond his makeshift cardboard shelter. The streets whispered secrets, and Billy became a silent detective among the city's forgotten.

As he roamed the city at night, Billy discovered a series of mysterious disappearances among the homeless population. Those who had once shared alleyways and makeshift campsites with him were gone without a trace. The city's officials dismissed it as a natural consequence of urban life, but Billy sensed something more sinister at play.

Billy's investigation led him to an underground network of tunnels beneath the city, where he stumbled upon a makeshift shelter for the disappeared homeless. Here, he uncovered a shocking truth – a government-backed initiative to clear the streets and sell the land to wealthy developers. The homeless people who were missing were being forcibly relocated to hidden facilities, their existence erased from public records.

Determined to expose the corruption, Billy reached out to a sympathetic journalist, Emma Turner, who saw the potential for a groundbreaking story. Together, they delved into the heart of the conspiracy, risking their lives to gather evidence and testimonies from those who had escaped the secret facilities.

As they closed in on the truth, Billy and Emma became targets. Shadows lurked around every corner, and mysterious figures tried to silence them. The city's dark underbelly fought back against the revelation of its secrets.

In a climactic confrontation, Billy and Emma presented their evidence to the public, revealing the extent of the corruption that preyed on the vulnerable homeless population. The city was shaken to its core as the truth unfolded, and the culprits were brought to justice.

Billy, once just another faceless figure in the city's underbelly, emerged as a hero among the homeless. His determination exposed the conspiracy and sparked a movement for change. The city was forced to confront its darker side, and as the dust settled, efforts were made to address the plight of the homeless and prevent further exploitation.

Having played a pivotal role in uncovering the truth, Billy chose to continue his life on the streets, forever vigilant for signs of injustice. The city may have ignored its homeless population, but Billy had shown that even those society deemed invisible could be the ones to unveil its deepest secrets.

Magical Wilma

Wilma's isolation began when a mysterious incident occurred on the day of her thirtieth birthday. People in the town started treating her with an odd mix of fear and awe. Whispers of a curse surrounded her name, and she became a pariah overnight. Friendships crumbled, job opportunities vanished, and Wilma found herself alone, with only the shadows as her companions.

One fateful evening, as the sun dipped below the horizon, casting a warm glow on the town, Wilma ventured into the woods that bordered the outskirts. She stumbled upon an ancient oak tree, its gnarled branches reaching out like skeletal fingers. The air was charged with an otherworldly energy, and Wilma felt an invisible force guiding her deeper into the forest.

Unknown to Wilma, the mystical force had chosen her – a guardian spirit that would help her navigate the challenges she faced and rediscover her place in society. From that moment, Wilma's life became a delicate dance between reality and the enchanting realm she had stumbled upon.

The guardian spirit manifested itself as a luminescent butterfly with iridescent wings. It fluttered around Wilma, guiding her with a gentle touch. As they embarked on this journey together, the once somber woman found a renewed sense of purpose.

One day, as Wilma meandered through the town square, the guardian spirit led her to a dilapidated bookstore tucked away in a forgotten corner. The shelves were dusty, and the air carried the musty scent of old paper. The shopkeeper, an elderly man with kind eyes, looked up from behind the counter as the bell above the door jingled.

"Ah, welcome, dear. Haven't seen a customer in years," he said, a hint of surprise in his voice.

Wilma felt drawn to a peculiar book on the top shelf, its cover adorned with symbols that seemed to pulse with energy. The guardian spirit glowed brighter as she opened it, and the pages revealed ancient spells and forgotten incantations. Wilma realized that her newfound companion was more than a guide; it was a conduit to a world where magic and reality intertwined.

With each spell she mastered, Wilma found herself changing. People no longer recoiled at her presence; instead, they were captivated by the charm that surrounded her. The guardian spirit's magic extended beyond the visible, touching hearts and minds breaking the shackles of prejudice that had bound her for so long.

Word of Wilma's transformation spread through the town like wildfire. Curiosity replaced fear, and soon, she became a sought-after figure. Both old and new friends reached out to her, drawn by the inexplicable allure that now surrounded her. The guardian spirit, always at her side, continued to guide her, its wings sparkling with a radiance that mirrored the newfound light in Wilma's life.

Emboldened by her magical journey, Wilma decided to confront the source of her isolation. The townspeople, once wary, now gathered in the square to witness the woman who had defied the supposed curse. Wilma addressed the crowd with the guardian spirit by her side, sharing her story and the magic that had transformed her.

The people listened, captivated by her words and the enchanting presence that surrounded her. Slowly, the veil of mistrust lifted, replaced by a shared sense of wonder. The guardian spirit fluttered above, casting a luminous glow that united the once-divided community.

As the sun set on that transformative day, Wilma stood in the center of the town square, surrounded by smiling faces and open hearts. The guardian spirit, content with its role as a catalyst for change, soared into the twilight sky, leaving behind a trail of stardust.

Wilma's journey had come full circle, and the town that had once shunned her now embraced her as one of their own. The bookstore, once forgotten, flourished with newfound life, and the magic within its pages continued to inspire others to break free from the chains of prejudice.

In the heart of the quaint town, where reality intertwined with the mystical, Wilma had discovered the enchanting power within herself and the magic that could bridge the gaps between people. The guardian spirit's influence lingered, reminding everyone that it sometimes took a touch of magic to unveil the beauty hidden within the ordinary.

Betty and Fred

In the heart of the city, where the skyline reached towards the heavens, Betty and Fred existed on the fringes of society. They were faces in the sea of anonymity; their stories woven into the fabric of the urban landscape. Behind the bustling streets and towering buildings, their tale unfolded, a poignant commentary on the pervasive issue of homelessness.

Betty, a middle-aged woman with faded dreams clinging to her like shadows, had once thrived in the corporate world. Yet, as fate would have it, a series of unfortunate events unfolded, leading to her descent into homelessness. The world outside her office had seemed distant, inconceivable. Now, cardboard walls and makeshift shelters defined her reality.

    Their paths converged beneath a flickering streetlamp one cold night, where they found solace in each other's company. United by circumstance, Betty and Fred formed an unlikely alliance, seeking warmth in the shared laughter that momentarily drowned out the harsh realities they faced.

Their journey unfolded against the backdrop of a city that never slept yet remained blind to the struggles of those who wandered its streets. The cold indifference of passersby echoed the societal attitudes towards the homeless – a blend of discomfort, apathy, and judgment. Betty and Fred were often reduced to mere statistics in a system that failed to acknowledge the complexity of their stories.

One day, as winter tightened its grip on the city, Betty and Fred found themselves seeking refuge in an abandoned building. The bitter wind seeped through the cracks in the walls, biting into their frail forms. As they huddled for warmth, Betty's eyes caught a flicker of hope in an old newspaper – a shelter was opening its doors to provide respite from the relentless cold.

Jack, the former factory Worker

In the early 1990s, against the backdrop of grunge music and the rise of the internet, the issue of homelessness in America had reached a critical juncture. The economic downturn and societal shifts had left many individuals adrift, their stories echoing through the forgotten corners of cities. During this time, Jack, a former factory worker, found himself on the unforgiving streets of Seattle.

Jack's descent into homelessness was swift, a casualty of factory closures and the shifting landscape of employment. The once-booming industrial town had become a ghost of its former self, leaving Jack without a job, a home, and a sense of purpose. As the recession tightened its grip, homelessness surged, and the challenges faced by people like Jack laid bare the inadequacies of existing social policies.

Jack huddled beneath a bridge one cold night, seeking refuge from the biting wind. There, he encountered Sarah, a social worker determined to make a difference in the lives of those abandoned by the system. Sarah, armed with empathy and an understanding of the evolving cultural landscape, recognized the need for a more nuanced approach to addressing homelessness.

Inspired by this changing tide, Sarah worked tirelessly to connect Jack with resources beyond the conventional shelters. She navigated the evolving social services network, collaborating with nonprofits and community organizations that sought to provide temporary relief and a pathway toward sustainable solutions.

In this era, cultural attitudes toward homelessness were also evolving. The prevalent stereotype of the homeless as solely individuals grappling with addiction or mental health issues was being challenged. Stories like Jack's highlighted the broader economic factors contributing to homelessness, shifting public perceptions, and prompting a call for systemic change.

As the 1990s progressed, the focus on "Housing First" initiatives gained traction. The idea was to prioritize providing stable housing as a foundation for addressing other challenges faced by the homeless population, such as mental health issues and unemployment. This approach signaled a departure from the traditional model that required individuals to meet certain criteria, such as sobriety, before accessing housing assistance.

Jack became a beneficiary of this evolving approach. With Sarah's assistance, he secured stable housing, a pivotal moment that marked the beginning of his journey toward rebuilding his life. The shelter he found was a temporary respite and a steppingstone towards self-sufficiency.

During this period, the federal government also played a role in shaping homelessness policies. The Stewart B. McKinney Homeless Assistance Act, initially enacted in the 1980s, was reauthorized in 1990, emphasizing the importance of collaboration between federal, state, and local entities in addressing homelessness. This legislation laid the groundwork for increased funding for shelters, outreach programs, and research on homelessness.

However, challenges persisted. The sheer scale of homelessness demanded continued innovation and a multi-pronged approach. Community-driven initiatives, often fueled by grassroots organizations, played a crucial role in advocating for the homeless and pushing for systemic changes.

The cultural shift was also reflected in popular media. Movies like "My Own Private Idaho" and "The Fisher King" portrayed nuanced narratives of homelessness, contributing to a more empathetic understanding of the issue. Musicians like Pearl Jam and Nirvana used their platforms to raise awareness about homelessness, adding their voices to the growing chorus advocating for change.

Jack's life had taken a positive turn as the decade drew to a close. He became an advocate for the homeless, sharing his experiences to humanize the issue and inspire change. Sarah continued her work, navigating the evolving landscape of social services, adapting to new policies, and pushing for even more comprehensive solutions.

The 1990s marked a pivotal era in the evolution of homelessness policies and cultural attitudes. Jack's journey exemplified the transformative power of a more compassionate and holistic approach, from the shadows of a Seattle bridge to the hopeful embrace of stable housing. The decade set the stage for further advancements in understanding homelessness, paving the way for ongoing efforts to address this complex societal challenge.

The Couple: Jim and Sally

The city hummed with life, an orchestra of footsteps, laughter, and the distant hum of traffic. Yet, amidst the symphony, Jim stood on a forgotten street corner, invisible to the bustling world around him. Once a factory worker with dreams as sturdy as the buildings that loomed above him, Jim found himself entangled in the unforgiving grip of homelessness.

His days were a routine of searching for scraps, each alley a potential haven, each discarded corner a possible shelter for the night. As the seasons changed, so did his world – the biting chill of winter, the scorching heat of summer, and the cool breeze that whispered the passage of time.

Today, as the sun dipped below the horizon, casting long shadows on the city's concrete canvas, Jim settled into a familiar alcove. Cardboard walls provided a fragile shield against the night's chill. The empty stomach gnawed, a reminder of unfulfilled dreams and unmet expectations. Yet, amidst the adversity, a glimmer of resilience lingered.

Sally's Perspective:

Sally navigated the city's vibrant streets with purpose, her steps fueled by a desire to make a difference. A social worker with a heart attuned to the silent pleas echoing through the alleys, Sally had seen the faces of homelessness – a mosaic of stories etched by hardship and resilience. Today, her mission led her to a corner where Jim sought refuge.

As she approached, Sally observed the man wrapped in layers of tattered clothing, his eyes reflecting the weariness of a life spent on the streets. She hesitated, aware of the delicate dance between offering help and respecting the autonomy of those she sought to assist.

"Hey there," Sally greeted gently, her voice a soothing melody amidst the city's cacophony.

Jim, startled from his thoughts, looked up. His eyes met hers, a fleeting connection in the vast expanse of urban solitude. Sally saw beyond the weathered exterior – a person with a history, dreams, and struggles etched into the lines on his face.

"I'm Sally. How's your day been?" she asked, recognizing the fragility of this moment.

Jim's response was initially guarded, a reflex honed by the harsh reality of life on the streets. Yet, as Sally persisted with genuine interest, a dialogue unfolded. Jim spoke of a life unraveled by job losses, economic downturns, and a series of unfortunate events that led him to this corner, this moment of intersection.

Jim's Perspective:

As the conversation unfolded, Jim found himself sharing more than just the surface of his story. He spoke of the dreams he had once cradled – a house with a white picket fence and a steady job to support a family. The threads of those dreams had unraveled, leaving him with fragments of a distant, almost surreal life.

Sally listened, not with pity, but with a profound empathy that transcended the boundaries of societal roles. She saw Jim not as a statistic but as a person whose journey had been marred by circumstances beyond his control. In her eyes, he was not defined by the cardboard walls that sheltered him but by the resilience that persisted within.

The exchange planted a seed of connection, a fragile bond between two individuals navigating the complexities of life. As Sally shared resources – a meal, information about nearby shelters, and avenues for employment assistance – Jim felt a spark of hope that had long eluded him.

Sally's Perspective:

Sally's encounters with individuals like Jim were not isolated acts of charity; they were a testament to her commitment to systemic change. As a social worker, she moved beyond the immediate alleviation of suffering, seeking avenues to address the root causes of homelessness. Advocacy for affordable housing, mental health resources, and comprehensive support systems became the pillars of her mission.

Her interactions with Jim, however, were a poignant reminder that change wasn't confined to legislative measures and policy reforms; it unfolded in the intimate spaces of human connection. The stories she heard the faces she encountered, became the driving force behind her relentless pursuit of a more compassionate society.

Jim's Perspective:

Days turned into weeks, and Sally's visits became a consistent thread in the tapestry of Jim's life. The cardboard walls began to crumble, not under the weight of despair but from the force of a burgeoning friendship. As Sally learned about Jim's skills – the craftsmanship he honed during his factory days – she saw beyond the limitations imposed by homelessness.

Together, they navigated the labyrinth of social services, seeking employment opportunities that aligned with Jim's abilities. The process was riddled with challenges, and the system's bureaucracy was often a formidable adversary. Yet, Sally's unwavering commitment and Jim's newfound hope forged a partnership that transcended the traditional boundaries of social work.

Sally's Perspective:

In the quiet moments between visits, Sally reflected on the transformative power of connection. The story of Jim was not an isolated incident; it echoed the broader narrative of systemic change. As she advocated for policies that addressed the multifaceted nature of homelessness, Sally recognized the importance of human stories in influencing societal attitudes.

She shared Jim's story through various platforms, emphasizing the resilience that persisted within individuals facing homelessness. The narrative became a catalyst for community-driven initiatives, inspiring others to look beyond stereotypes and embrace a more empathetic understanding of the issue.

Jim's Perspective:

The turning point came when a local business, inspired by Sally's advocacy and Jim's skills, offered him a part-time job. It wasn't just a paycheck but a symbol of a community that chose to uplift rather than cast aside. The warmth of a shared workspace replaced the cardboard walls, and Jim found himself on a path toward self-sufficiency.

Jim and Sally's intersection became a beacon of hope in the intricate dance between adversity and compassion. Jim, once defined by the shadows of homelessness, emerged as a testament to the transformative power of human connection. Sally, driven by a steadfast commitment to change, witnessed the tangible impact of her advocacy on an individual level.

Though humble in the vast expanse of urban narratives, their journey illuminated the nuanced layers of addressing homelessness – the importance of systemic change intertwined with the intimate moments of empathy, understanding, and shared humanity. As Jim found his way back into the fabric of society, the intersection of their lives lingered as a reminder that connection and compassion could redefine destinies in the face of adversity.

Teenage Jason

In the heart of the city, where towering skyscrapers cast long shadows overcrowded streets, lived a young soul named Jason. At the age of fifteen, life had dealt him a hand that no one his age should be forced to play. His world crumbled when his parents succumbed to the weight of financial burdens, leaving him with nothing but a backpack and the harsh reality of homelessness.

Jason's journey into the unknown began with the echo of his footsteps against the cold pavement. Each night, he sought refuge in the quiet corners of the city, where the flickering streetlights painted fleeting patterns on the concrete canvas. In those silent moments, Jason grappled with questions that transcended his teenage years – questions of identity, belonging, and the elusive concept of finding one's place in the world.

As days turned into nights, Jason discovered that survival was more than just navigating the streets; it was a profound journey of self-discovery. The reflection in store windows became a silent companion, a reminder of the boy who once had a home, dreams, and a sense of belonging. Now, in the anonymity of the urban landscape, he faced the challenge of shaping his identity amid the shadows.

The city's underbelly became Jason's classroom, teaching him lessons that no textbook could convey. He learned the art of resourcefulness, scavenging for food in dumpsters and finding warmth in abandoned buildings. He discovered the unwritten rules of the streets – the silent camaraderie among the homeless, the transient alliances forged in the struggle for survival.

Jason's journey of self-discovery took an unexpected turn when he encountered a community of fellow souls navigating the harsh landscape of homelessness. Among them, he found a sense of belonging that transcended societal norms. Each person brought a unique story, a complex tapestry woven with threads of struggle, resilience, and survival.

In the heart of the makeshift community, Jason met Maya, a wise and warm-hearted woman who had weathered storms of her own. She became a mentor, guiding him through the intricacies of life on the streets and offering wisdom that extended beyond mere survival. Maya saw potential in Jason, a spark that could reignite the dreams he thought he had lost forever.

Together, they faced the daily challenges of homelessness – the constant threat of eviction from makeshift shelters, the search for sustenance, and the invisible battle against societal judgments. Maya became a beacon of hope in Jason's life, encouraging him to embrace his identity and flaws.

As the seasons changed, so did Jason. The boy who once roamed the city streets with uncertainty began to assert his presence in the world. He found solace in the simple pleasures – a warm meal from a local shelter, a shared story around a makeshift bonfire, and genuine camaraderie among those who knew his struggles.

One day, as the sun painted the sky with hues of orange and pink, Maya handed Jason a journal. Its empty pages beckoned him to pour his thoughts onto the canvas of words. Through hesitant strokes of the pen, Jason found his voice – a narrative that chronicled the challenges, the victories, and the profound journey of self-discovery that unfolded beneath the city's indifferent skyline.

The journal became a testament to Jason's resilience and the power of identity forged in the crucible of adversity. In Maya's eyes, he saw not just a homeless teenager but a young soul brimming with potential. The city, which had once seemed like an imposing labyrinth, now held the promise of opportunity.

As the years passed, Jason's narrative took a new turn. Through Maya's guidance and the strength, he found within himself, he secured a part-time job and enrolled in a local school for homeless youth. The streets, which had once defined his identity, now became a distant memory – a chapter in his life that shaped him but did not define him.

In the graduation ceremony that marked a new chapter in his life, Jason stood on the stage with a diploma in hand. The cheers of fellow graduates, the proud smiles of mentors, and the warmth of Maya's gaze painted a portrait of victory against the odds. With its towering skyscrapers, the city stood as a backdrop to a story of identity reclaimed and a place found in the world.

Jason's coming-of-age tale was not just about homelessness; it was a testament to the resilience of the human spirit, the power of community, and the transformative journey of self-discovery. As he looked towards the horizon, the once-daunting cityscape now held the promise of endless possibilities. The boy who had faced the harsh reality of the streets emerged not broken but stronger, a testament to the enduring power of hope and the indomitable human will.

Alex the Advocate

Alex, a once-successful software engineer, found himself in the midst of a future dystopia. The allure of technological advancements had lured him into a world of virtual realities and augmented dreams, but an unexpected turn of events had stripped him of everything. Jobless, disconnected, and cast aside by a society immersed in its digital utopia, Alex became one of the countless souls wandering the streets.

In this future reality, homelessness has taken on new dimensions. The traditional image of makeshift shelters and cardboard boxes had given way to a transient existence within the digital ether. Those without a physical address were now the ghosts of the metropolis, wandering through the augmented landscapes of the city's underbelly.

Alex roamed the streets, his physical presence invisible to the bustling crowds engrossed in their augmented realities.

The city's skyscrapers towered over him, their shimmering surfaces reflecting the stark contrast between the haves and the have-nots. His once state-of-the-art knowledge in software engineering now felt obsolete in a world driven by algorithms and artificial intelligence.

As Alex meandered through the digital shadows, he encountered others like him who had fallen through the cracks of progress. In this future society, the homeless population formed an unseen community, sharing virtual spaces where they sought solace and connection in the midst of their shared adversity.

The streets were alive with whispered conversations and silent camaraderie. Beneath the neon glow of holographic billboards, they exchanged tales of the world they once knew and the one that had left them behind. Alex became part of this invisible tapestry, finding refuge in the intangible bonds forged within the digital realm.

One day, Alex stumbled upon an abandoned server room hidden beneath the labyrinth of the city's infrastructure. It became a clandestine sanctuary for the digital homeless – a space where they could temporarily escape the isolation of their augmented existence and connect with others who shared their struggles.

In this hidden realm, Alex discovered a mentor named Elena, a former data scientist who once contributed to the technologies that had rendered her homeless. Elena saw potential in Alex's dormant skills and sought to harness the power of the digital world to address the challenges faced by their community.

Together, they embarked on a mission to leverage their knowledge of the digital landscape to create platforms that could connect the homeless to resources and opportunities. They became architects of change within the hidden realms of cyberspace, crafting virtual bridges that spanned the gaps in the physical world.

As the digital homeless community grew, so did their influence. They orchestrated virtual protests against the systemic issues that perpetuated homelessness, leveraging their collective knowledge to expose the disparities and injustices that lurked within the city's shiny exterior.

In response, a group of activists within the augmented reality community joined forces with Alex and Elena. Together, they initiated a movement to bridge the divide between the digital and physical realms, advocating for recognizing the homeless population and creating innovative solutions that addressed their unique challenges.

The movement gained traction, and the digital homeless became a force to be reckoned with in the struggle for societal change. Their stories echoed through the virtual corridors, penetrating the consciousness of a society that had long overlooked their existence. The augmented reality developers began incorporating features that aimed to address the needs of the homeless, creating virtual shelters and job-search platforms accessible to those without a physical address.

As the movement gained momentum, the city's skyline underwent a different transformation. The gleaming towers of progress now reflected a society awakening to the realities of its marginalized members. Affordable housing initiatives, mental health resources, and job training programs became integral components of the city's response to homelessness.

In this transformed reality, Alex found himself at the forefront of change. Once a clandestine refuge, the abandoned server room now symbolized resilience and innovation. Alex, Elena, and the digital homeless community had become pioneers in reshaping societal attitudes towards those who had fallen through the gaps in progress.

The movement sparked a domino effect, prompting cities around the world to reevaluate their approaches to homelessness. The integration of technology and a renewed focus on empathy and inclusivity paved the way for a future where no one was left behind in the wake of progress.

For Alex, the journey from homelessness to advocacy marked a coming-of-age in a world defined by its digital landscapes and augmented realities. The invisible bonds forged within the hidden realms of cyberspace had transcended the confines of the virtual, shaping a future where the homeless were not just statistics but individuals with stories, dreams, and the resilience to rebuild their lives. Once a desolate battleground, the streets became avenues of hope and transformation, echoing with the footsteps of those who had navigated the complexities of a future where homelessness had taken on new dimensions.

Dave the Comedian

The bustling streets of the city seemed indifferent to Dave's plight. A disheveled figure with a worn-out hat, Dave shuffled through the urban jungle with a sense of humor that defied his circumstances. Once a stand-up comedian with dreams of making it big, life's twists had landed him on the streets.

Dave's days were an unpredictable blend of comedic survival tactics. He had mastered the art of turning discarded cardboard boxes into makeshift stand-up stages, entertaining the city's passersby with jokes that echoed between the towering buildings. His comedic spirit, a resilient flame in the face of adversity, was the beacon that guided him through the harsh realities of homelessness.

As Lisa laughed, she saw beyond the comedic facade. Dave's eyes held a certain sadness, a depth that hinted at a journey marked by unexpected detours. Intrigued by the man who turned his hardships into humor, Lisa decided to explore Dave's story, hoping to shed light on the often-overlooked humanity within the homeless population.

Over the next few days, Lisa accompanied Dave on his urban adventures, witnessing the comedic survival strategies he employed. From creating a "spa day" in a public fountain to turning a dumpster-diving escapade into a culinary critique, Dave's comedic genius transcended the confines of his circumstances.

Lisa's articles on Dave garnered attention, painting a heartfelt portrait of a man who used humor as a shield against the harshness of reality. The city responded with a mix of laughter and empathy, and Dave's cardboard comedy routine became a local sensation.

As Dave performed his routine one day, an unexpected guest appeared in the audience – a talent scout named Maggie. Intrigued by the charismatic homeless comedian, Maggie saw potential beyond the cardboard stage. She approached Dave with an offer that seemed straight out of a sitcom.

"Dave, how about bringing your comedy to a real stage? I run a small comedy club downtown, and I think you'd be a hit with our audience," Maggie suggested.

Dave, initially skeptical, found himself standing on a legitimate stage that evening, bathed in the warm glow of stage lights instead of the flickering neon of the city. The audience, a mix of curious locals and loyal fans, eagerly awaited his performance. Dave took a deep breath, his worn-out hat replaced by a borrowed fedora that added a theatrical flair.

As Dave delivered his routine, the laughter echoed through the club, filling the room with a contagious joy. It wasn't just a comedic act but a testament to the resilience of the human spirit. The following applause marked a turning point for Dave, a homeless man who had if only for a moment, found solace and acceptance in the spotlight.

The comedic success, however, brought its own set of challenges. Now balancing the demands of both cardboard comedy and traditional stand-up, Dave faced a dilemma that tested the delicate balance between humor and authenticity. Lisa, who had become a friend and confidante, noticed the strain on Dave's shoulders.

"Dave, don't lose yourself in the pursuit of laughter. Your authenticity is what makes your comedy so special," Lisa advised one evening as they sat on a park bench, city lights twinkling in the background.

Dave pondered Lisa's words, realizing that his journey had become more than just a comedic escapade. While shining brightly, the spotlight cast shadows on the vulnerabilities he had masked with humor. It was time to address the underlying issues that had led him to the streets in the first place.

With Lisa's support, Dave embarked on a journey of self-discovery. Comedy became a therapeutic outlet, a way to explore and share the complexities of his experiences. The laughter remained, but now it resonated with a depth that touched the hearts of those who listened.

One day, as Dave performed a new routine that blended humor with introspection, a surprise guest – Dave's estranged family appeared in the audience. The unexpected reunion unfolded with laughter and tears, a poignant reminder that the journey back into society was sometimes paved with comedic and dramatic twists.

Dave's return to the familial fold became a symbol of hope for many who faced similar struggles. His comedy, now infused with a blend of humor and heartfelt narratives, resonated on a deeper level. The city, which had once been a backdrop for his cardboard stage, now embraced him as both a comedian and a survivor.

The city, forever changed by the laughter that echoed through its streets, became a canvas where Dave painted his narrative – a narrative that showcased the transformative power of humor in the face of adversity. Once an invisible soul navigating the shadows of homelessness, Dave had found his place in the world as a comedian and storyteller whose laughter touched the hearts of a city that learned to see beyond the cardboard and embrace the authenticity within.

12

THE FUTURE OF HOMELESSNESS IN AMERICA

Progress Made and Challenges Ahead

Over the past few decades, there has been some progress made in addressing the issue of homelessness in America. The implementation of programs such as Housing First, which prioritize providing stable housing for individuals experiencing homelessness, has shown promising results in reducing the overall number of homeless individuals in the country. Additionally, increased awareness and advocacy efforts have helped to shed light on the root causes of homelessness, such as lack of affordable housing, mental health issues, and substance abuse.

However, despite these advancements, there are still many challenges ahead in addressing the issue of homelessness in America. One of the biggest challenges is the lack of affordable housing options for low-income individuals and families. The rising cost of housing in many cities across the country has made it increasingly difficult for those living on the margins to find stable and safe housing. This is further exacerbated by the lack of funding for affordable housing programs and the limited availability of resources for those experiencing homelessness.

Another major challenge facing the homeless population in America is the stigma and discrimination they often face. Many homeless individuals report feeling invisible and marginalized by society, which can make it even more difficult for them to access the resources and support they need to get back on their feet. It is crucial for all Americans to recognize the humanity and dignity of those experiencing homelessness and to work towards creating a more inclusive and supportive society for all.

In order to address these challenges, it is essential for policymakers, advocates, and community members to come together to develop comprehensive solutions to homelessness in America. This includes increasing funding for affordable housing programs, expanding access to mental health and substance abuse treatment services, and addressing systemic issues such as poverty and income inequality. By working together and prioritizing the needs of the homeless population, we can make meaningful progress towards ending homelessness in America once and for all. It is time for all Americans to come together and take action to ensure that everyone has a safe and stable place to call home.

Building a More Equitable and Compassionate Society

Building a more equitable and compassionate society is essential in addressing the struggles faced by the homeless population in America. It is important for all Americans to recognize the humanity and dignity of those experiencing homelessness and to work towards creating a more inclusive and supportive society for all individuals. By fostering a sense of empathy and understanding, we can begin to break down the stigmas and stereotypes that often perpetuate the cycle of homelessness.

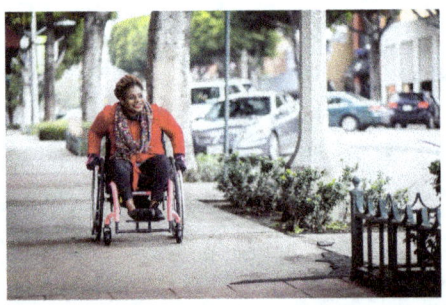

One way to build a more equitable society is by advocating for policies that prioritize affordable housing and support services for the homeless. This includes increasing funding for shelters, transitional housing programs, and mental health services, as well as implementing policies that address the root causes of homelessness, such as poverty, lack of affordable healthcare, and systemic inequality. By investing in these resources, we can provide a pathway to stability and independence for those experiencing homelessness.

In addition to policy changes, individuals can also play a role in building a more compassionate society by volunteering their time and resources to support homeless individuals in their communities. This can include donating to local shelters, participating in outreach programs, or simply taking the time to engage in meaningful conversations with those experiencing homelessness. By showing kindness and empathy towards others, we can create a more inclusive and supportive community for all individuals.

It is also important for Americans to educate themselves about the complexities of homelessness and to challenge their own biases and assumptions. By learning about the diverse experiences and challenges faced by the homeless population, we can begin to break down barriers and foster a greater sense of understanding and empathy. This can help to create a more inclusive society where all individuals are valued and supported, regardless of their housing status.

Ultimately, building a more equitable and compassionate society requires a collective effort from all Americans. By working together to address the systemic issues that contribute to homelessness and by fostering a sense of empathy and understanding towards those experiencing homelessness, we can create a more just and compassionate society for all individuals. It is only through a shared commitment to social justice and equality that we can truly make a difference in the lives of the homeless population in America.

A Call to Action for All Americans

As Americans, we are faced with a crisis that is often overlooked and ignored - the issue of homelessness in our country. It is time for us to come together and take action to address this pressing issue that affects so many of our fellow citizens. The homeless in America are often invisible, living on the streets or in shelters, struggling to survive day to day. It is our moral responsibility to ensure that every American has access to safe and stable housing.

We cannot continue to turn a blind eye to the plight of the homeless in America. It is time for us to step up and make a difference in the lives of those who are most vulnerable in our society. We must advocate for affordable housing, mental health services, and job training programs that can help lift people out of homelessness and into a better life. It is not enough to simply provide temporary solutions - we must work towards long-term, sustainable solutions that address the root causes of homelessness.

It is easy to feel overwhelmed by the magnitude of the homelessness crisis in America, but we must remember that change starts with individual actions. Whether it is volunteering at a homeless shelter, donating to organizations that support the homeless, or advocating for policy changes at the local and national levels, each of us has the power to make a difference. We must come together as a community and support our homeless neighbors in their time of need.

The homeless in America are not a faceless statistic - they are our friends, our family members, our neighbors. We must treat them with compassion and dignity, and work towards creating a society where everyone has a place to call home. It is time for us to take a stand and say enough is enough - homelessness is not a problem that can be ignored any longer. Let us come together as Americans and work towards a future where every person has a roof over their head and a chance at a better life.

Invisible in America: The Struggle of the Homeless is a call to action for all Americans. It is a reminder that we have a responsibility to our fellow citizens, especially those who are most vulnerable. Let us come together, united in our efforts to end homelessness in America and create a more just and compassionate society for all.

One Solution to Help Homeless Americans
Build Tiny Houses on government-owned or purchased land.

It's disheartening to observe that individuals arriving without a credit history can secure Small Business Administration (SBA) loans and establish businesses more easily than their American counterparts with challenging credit histories. This stark reality raises questions about the fairness of our systems.

Even more concerning is the juxtaposition of living conditions. Immigrants, even those closely monitored by Border

Patrol in states like Arizona, California, and Texas, seem to enjoy better accommodations than Americans enduring homelessness. While our fellow citizens struggle beneath bridges, underpasses, and makeshift camps in the heart of our largest cities, they are unable to find an affordable, clean, and sanitary place to call home.

While acknowledging the issue's complexity, taking incremental steps at a governmental level could alleviate this nationwide problem, offering tangible relief to struggling Americans. The United States perpetually grapples with crises in providing adequate care for its citizens, and it's time to embark on a transformative initiative.

Tiny Houses is a simple yet powerful solution to lift our fellow Americans off the streets. In the face of an overwhelming problem, this proposal represents a tangible and compassionate response. Let's come together to make this a reality—it's the very least we can do to restore dignity and hope to those in need. By addressing the immediate crisis of homelessness, we can pave the way for a more compassionate and equitable society, one tiny house at a time.

13

CONCLUSION

Chapter 13 Conclusion

In conclusion, it is important for Americans to approach the issue of homelessness with empathy and compassion, rather than judgment and prejudice. By recognizing the humanity of individuals experiencing homelessness and working towards solutions that address the systemic issues at play, we can create a more inclusive and supportive society for all.

   Mental illness and substance abuse are significant challenges facing the homeless population in America. By understanding the complex interplay between these issues and advocating for improved access to mental health and addiction services, we can help break the cycle of homelessness and support those in need. As a society, it is our responsibility to ensure that all individuals have the resources and support they need to overcome their mental health challenges and build a brighter future for themselves .

Homeless shelters and support services are a crucial lifeline for those experiencing homelessness in America. These shelters provide a safe haven, resources, and support for individuals in need. As Americans, it is our duty to support and advocate for these vital services to ensure that everyone has access to the help they need. Together, we can work towards ending homelessness and creating a more equitable society for all.

While government programs and policies play a crucial role in addressing homelessness in America, there is still much work to be done. It is essential for policymakers, advocates, and community members to work together to ensure that homeless individuals have access to the resources and support they need to secure stable housing and improve their lives. By continuing to prioritize the needs of the homeless population and advocating for effective solutions, we can work towards ending homelessness in America once and for all.

Volunteering and donating are essential tools in the fight against homelessness in America. By giving our time, resources, and support to those in need, we can help to create a more just and equitable society for all. Let us all commit to making a difference in the lives of the homeless population by volunteering, donating, and advocating for positive change in our communities. Together, we can work towards ending homelessness and building a brighter future for all Americans.

People Need help!

THANK YOU FOR READING MY BOOK.

Hopefully, it helps you show more empathy to those you see on the streets.

Be Kind. Every one is fighting some kind of battle.

ABOUT THE AUTHOR

The Story of Susie Payne

Hi there! I'm Susie Payne and I hail from a small town in NJ. One of the most impactful experiences during my military service was gaining a profound understanding of the challenges faced by all Americans. Witnessing the resilience and strength of those who, for various reasons, found themselves in dire crisis' touched my heart. It ignited a passion within me to make a difference and be a voice for those who often go unheard. Today, I channel my experiences and empathy into various community initiatives in North Carolina. In my free time, you'll find me enjoying the simple pleasures of life – spending time with my own family, writing, reading, and exploring the beautiful outdoors.

www.ingramcontent.com/pod-product-compliance
Lightning Source LLC
LaVergne TN
LVHW021952060526
838201LV00049B/1678